Who's Stealing Your Business ?

Who's Stealing Your Business ?

How to Identify and Prevent Business Espionage

William Johnson
with
Jack Maguire

amacom
American Management Association

This book is available at a special
discount when ordered in bulk quantities.
For information, contact Special Sales Department,
AMACOM, a division of American Management Association,
135 West 50th Street, New York, NY 10020.

Library of Congress Cataloging-in-Publication Data

Johnson, William, 1934–
  Who's stealing your business?

  Includes index.
  1. Business intelligence—Prevention. 2. Industry
—Security measures. I. Maguire, Jack. II. Title.
HD38.7.J64   1988   658.4'72   88–47711
ISBN 0–8144–5903–X

Following is a list of sources of incidents and court cases mentioned in this book:

The Great Cookie Caper, pages 1–2: Manuel Schiffres and Gail Bronson, "Businesses Struggle to Keep Their Secrets," *U. S. News & World Report*, Sept. 23, 1985, p. 59.

The Hanson incident, page 2: Richard Eells and Peter Nehemkis, *Corporate Intelligence and Espionage* (New York: Macmillan, 1984), p. 113.

The Dr. Aries incident, page 2: Richard Eells and Peter Nehemkis, *Corporate Intelligence and Espionage* (New York: Macmillan, 1984), pp. 116–117.

Du Pont versus the aerial photographers, pages 2–3: Rod Willis, "Corporate Cloaks and Daggers," *Management Review*, Feb. 1986, p. 41.

Kellogg's decision not to allow tour groups, page 3: Alan D. Haas, "Corporate Cloak and Dagger," *Amtrak Express*, Oct./Nov. 1986, p. 19.

Hertz versus Joseph V. Vittoria, page 3: Clemens P. Work, "When a Key Worker Leaves With Secrets," *U. S. News & World Report*, Oct. 7, 1985, p. 67.

Thomas' accusations against Entenmann's, page 3: Alan D. Haas, "Corporate Cloak and Dagger," *Amtrak Express*, Oct./Nov. 1986, p. 19.

Japanese executives accused of stealing IBM computer blueprints and codes, page 18: David E. Sanger, "IBM and Hitachi in New Accord," *New York Times*, Nov. 12, 1986, p. D1.

The Hillenbrand saga, pages 19–21: Robert Johnson, "Inside Job: The Case of Marc Feith Shows Corporate Spies Aren't Just High Tech," *Wall Street Journal*, Jan. 9, 1987, p. 1.

Printing number

10   9   8   7   6   5   4   3   2   1

What This Book Will Do for You

When most people hear the word "espionage," they conjure up exotic images: James Bond tailing a revolutionary anarchist across the Australian outback in his custom-built Lamborghini, or Mata Hari seducing a corrupt general in the inner sanctum of the French War Ministry. They seldom think in terms of an accountant rummaging through a trash dumpster for rough drafts of his co-worker's new proposal, or of a part-time clerk loitering outside a conference room to catch start-up dates for a competitor, or of a junior vice-president making photocopies of her soon-to-be ex-employer's files so she can take them to her new job. Nevertheless, these last three images are far more representative of the most pervasive and costly form of espionage—business espionage.

In fact, espionage is *not* exotic at all! By undermining the economic productivity of this country as a whole, corporate spying touches the life of each and every business and businessperson in America. In October 1987, the Maryland Center for Business Management (MCBM) reported that American companies lose over $50 billion a year as a result of espionage. And the menace strikes every kind of organization, be it big or little, high-tech or low-tech, industrial or service, professional or trade, profit or nonprofit. Ann Grille, a reporter for *Fortune* magazine, claims that 20 percent of the upper-level executives in *Fortune* 500 companies are either spies or victims of spies, and the MCBM study estimates that one-third of all new businesses fail because of dishonest employees.

Business espionage thrives on the fact that people misunderstand it, or underestimate it, or choose to ignore it. As we proceed through the 1990s, however, it will be increasingly difficult to avoid dealing with the problem. We are destined to witness an explosive growth in the range and power of business espionage, for the three major reasons that follow:

■ *Reason number one:* In our era the gathering and analysis of intelligence is rapidly replacing marketing as the driving force in business. Experts call this era the "Information Age." Information is easy to store, to disseminate, and to manipulate. Unfortunately, information is also easy to steal. The more the value of a company is tied up in its data banks, the more vulnerable the company is to being ripped off, and the costlier the ripoff can be. The average bank holdup totals $4,000, while the average computer crime totals more than $40,000. Large conglomerates already realize the gravity of the situation. IBM, for example, now invests around $60 million a year in counterespionage. Small outfits, which, because of their naiveté, are in many ways even more attractive victims, will have to follow IBM's lead to survive.

■ *Reason number two:* The advance of technology has far outstripped our ability to control it. Relatively inexpensive solid-state gadgetry now makes everyone a potential spy. Dak Industries Inc. alone claims to have more than 1.6 million customers and offers such sophisticated mail-order items as pocket copy machines and audio telescopes that can pick one voice out of a distant crowd. These easily operated tools, along with many other similar devices, can be legally sold to anyone. They can also be illegally used by anyone.

■ *Reason number three* (the most frightening of all): An increasingly competitive job market has severely eroded workplace ethics—a fact that no one in America has been able to ignore, thanks to the recent news coverage surrounding insider-trading scandals. The U.S. Bureau of Justice Statistics tells us that white collar crime *convictions* increased by 18 percent from 1980 to 1985 (the last period for which such statistics are available). A poll of senior business executives conducted in January 1988 by *Security* magazine states that 66 percent of the respondents think most people are unethical in their business dealings! As more and more people who enter the business world are trained either by example or by default to do whatever they can to get ahead in life, business espionage will inevitably mushroom into a far more common practice than it already is.

Today, detecting, controlling, and combating business espionage have clearly become the responsibility of *every* manager and executive in the business world—not just that of the designated security manager. If you want to maintain an honest and productive workplace, you cannot afford to ignore an escalating danger that directly threatens you, the people who report to you, and the people to whom you report. The odds are high that you are the victim, the dupe, or the legally liable agent of at least one espionage campaign right now!

Who's Stealing Your Business? has been specially designed to increase your understanding of how corporate spying works and to help you cope successfully with any espionage activity aimed at your office, factory, or home environment. It recognizes that spying is often indistinguishable from simple thievery. As such, it is the first book to combine security issues with business espionage controls and countermeasures, and it does so in a practical manner that can be put to immediate use by you, the reader. Within these pages, you will discover how to:

- Identify spy operations—what spies' methods, tools, and disguises are, plus what leads them to spying in the first place.
- Determine whether you may be a target or pawn of business espionage.
- Conduct step-by-step, do-it-yourself security surveys of your office, factory, and home environment.
- Take concrete action to protect your office, factory, and home environment from the threat of espionage.
- Manage effectively any crises that are caused by espionage.
- Enlist professional help to make your working environment safer in general and/or to solve a specific security or espionage problem.
- Supervise a professional undercover operation.
- Draw the line between legitimate research and spying, in terms of your own business conduct and the conduct of others.
- Establish ethics policies and procedures in your area of responsibility.
- Establish security goals, espionage controls, and countermeasures that best suit you, your co-workers, and your company.
- Motivate your employees to become safer, more honest, and more responsive to the threat of business espionage.

Who's Stealing Your Business? helps you to help yourself. Based on my thirty years of management and field experience in the war against business espionage, this book offers techniques and strategies that have already worked for other managers and that can easily be customized to work for you. It will open your eyes to a mysterious, danger-laden world that lies hidden all about you. And it will equip you to handle what you see.

Contents

CHAPTER 1

Mind Your Own Business:

A Look at the Problem of Business Espionage

> "Things may come to those
> who wait, but only the things
> left by those who hustle."
> **Abraham Lincoln**

Journalists called it the Great Cookie Caper when the news broke late in 1984. Procter & Gamble, proud producer of Duncan Hines home-style chocolate chip cookies, was accusing Nabisco, Keebler, and Frito-Lay of spying to steal the secret of P&G's "crispy outside, chewy inside" baking process. The three suits, assigned to U.S. District Court Judge Joseph J. Lombardi in New York, charged that the rival firms had engaged in espionage at sales presentations and at the baking plants themselves and were now using P&G's patented technique to make "infringing cookies." One suit cited an incident where a "spy plane" had actually flown over a P&G facility that was under construction!

Frito-Lay, the maker of Grandma's Rich 'n Chewy cookies, was quick to countersue. It denied most of the charges, but did confess that it had sent a worker to photograph the outside of a Duncan Hines plant. Unfortunately, the worker's college-age son had decided to act on his own: He had entered the plant and walked out with some unbaked dough. Frito-Lay insisted in court that it had thrown out both the dough and the pictures without looking at them and had even sent P&G an apology. P&G responded that the note had come only after the spy's hands had been, as it were, caught in the cookie jar. All cases are still active,

a principal stumbling block being terminology—the legal definition of "cookie" as well as the legal definition of "espionage"!

The Great Cookie Caper received a lot of publicity because
the brand names were familiar and because the public could laugh
at it. What is not "news" at all to most savvy businesspeople is
that the corporate world is full of spies. It always has been. Lately,
however, business espionage has grown to epidemic proportions,
and that's nothing to laugh about. In a dishonest marketplace,
everyone is the victim. Consider these other recent cases involving
high-profile corporations:

■ In the late 1970s Harold Hanson, an employee of a small
record manufacturer called Laurie Visual Etudes Inc., invented a
device for teaching students of wind instruments how to inhale
and exhale properly. Chesebrough-Ponds' health division learned
of Hanson's invention and expressed interest in obtaining a licens-
ing agreement to market the breath exerciser. Its own device for
patients with lung problems was much more difficult to use.

At Chesebrough's request, Hanson provided detailed drawings and prototypes of the breath exerciser. R&D people at Chesebrough promptly copied the design and used it as the basis of two
new products, Unifo and Triflo, which earned $13.5 million in
their first five years on the market. Hanson eventually won a settlement.

■ In 1985, Merck & Company, Rohm & Haas, and Sprague
Electric Company each accused Dr. Robert S. Aries, a well-
respected chemist who taught at Brooklyn Polytechnic Institute, of
operating a spy ring that used his graduate students as secret
agents. It seems the students were urged to bring their employers'
trade secrets to Dr. Aries as part of a "real-life test." The suing
companies claimed that Dr. Aries obtained "secret documents and
samples of extreme value" from the vaults of each company.

■ The same year that Dr. Aries was exposed, Du Pont discovered that a competitor had hired two aerial photographers to take
telephoto pictures of a new methanol plant Du Pont was building.
Lawyers for Du Pont successfully demonstrated during a court suit
against the photographers that an analysis of the photographs
could, indeed, disclose the nature of the secret formula for producing the alcohol derivative.

Although the photographers claimed the "right of public airspace" and refused to name their client, Judge Irving Goldberg of the U.S. Court of Appeals in New Orleans found in Du Pont's favor, saying, "This is a case of industrial espionage in which an airplane is the cloak and a camera, the dagger. . . . In taking this position we realize that industrial espionage of the sort here perpetrated has become a popular sport, but it is not to be condoned!"

■ In 1986 Kellogg Company in Battle Creek, Michigan, ended a beloved eighty-year tradition by barring tour groups. The decision came after security consultants caught spies from European cereal makers posing as tourists in order to steal new technology.

■ Also in 1986 Hertz filed suit against its former president Joseph V. Vittoria, who had gone on to become head of its archrival, Avis. Among other allegations, Hertz said that Vittoria had taken confidential documents with him when he left. Before everyone's dirty linen could be aired in court, the suit was settled.

■ In a similar 1986 case, Thomas' accused Entenmann's of sponsoring an undercover operation to find out how Thomas' made the famous "nooks and crannies" in its English muffins. The company based its claim on information that came to light when several key employees abruptly left to join Entenmann's. Again, an out-of-court settlement was reached before the mouth-watering details could be revealed.

August Bequai, an attorney and security expert based in Washington, D.C., sums up the current situation well: "Little companies steal from big companies, big companies steal from little companies, everybody steals from everybody. Anything is available for a price, particularly in a nation where nonviolent, white collar crimes are viewed somewhat indulgently."

In the simplest terms, business espionage refers to any illegal, unauthorized, or downright sneaky gathering of a company's information or material. The spy might be a professional spy-for-hire working for a competitor, for a disgruntled employee, or for someone who merely stands to gain from whatever is stolen. The spy might be a semiprofessional: a company employee who is being paid by someone else to steal company secrets or goods. Or the spy might be a complete amateur with a cause to promote, an ax to grind, a need to satisfy, or just an overactive curiosity to indulge.

Every statistic on the subject confirms that the population of all three spy categories is booming. According to a 1984 U.S. Department of Justice study, American industries lose $67 billion a year to internal crime and theft, almost double the estimate in a similar study made in 1979. A 1986 survey conducted by Information Data Search in Cambridge, Massachusetts, and reported in *Security* magazine, found that 80 percent of the top U.S. companies had been forced to increase their intelligence budgets dramatically over the previous three years. In a random sampling of its subscribers at the end of 1986, *Security* magazine learned that 58 percent had registered a sharper-than-ever increase in white collar crime since 1980, and 42 percent had noted "significant jumps" in computer crime specifically.

BUSINESS SPIES COMPARED WITH GOVERNMENT SPIES

In many respects, business espionage is much like government espionage, except that business espionage is most likely even more widespread and more intense. In the United States the distinction between the government spy and the corporate spy has almost disappeared over the last half-century, thanks to World War II, the Korean War, and the Vietnam conflict. In each of these, the government trained a huge number of spies (either newly recruited or "borrowed" from the underworld) and later turned them loose in the private sector, where they popularized new, more sophisticated spy methodologies.

The fact that the changeover from government to private spy, or vice versa, can be accomplished fairly easily should not be surprising. A pioneer in electronic countermeasures equipment once stated, "The goal of a successful industrial operation is the same as foreign espionage: to continually siphon off secrets without arousing the suspicions of the victim."

Spies in government and spies in business also exhibit a similar kind of defense mechanism: They hide their spy work behind a smoke screen of rationalizations. Typically, they cite a higher loyalty as a reason for their acts. If they must sometimes go against their moral precepts, they excuse it as "good in the long run." They are quick to point to the other side, making such statements as "Other people do it, so we must too." One of the major problems in combating either government spies or business spies is that they often believe, or come to believe, what they say—that the work they do is justified.

Americans can't help but be keenly aware of a growing public and private climate of amorality, one that encourages spying and threatens to undermine basic human rights. Since Watergate, private citizens of the United States have become increasingly disturbed by what they see as an invasion of their personal privacy. When asked by a 1986 Gallup poll if they thought existing protection-of-privacy laws were routinely broken, 85 percent of the respondents said they were certain that such activities as illegal wiretapping and electronic surveillance were going on in business and government all the time. Half of those interviewed thought that business or government agents would not hesitate to make improper use of the personal information they gathered. If the poll had focused on the business world in particular, the figures would no doubt have reflected even greater concern.

Regrettably, business espionage has increased far beyond the capacities of corporate security departments to handle it on their own. All company managers and executives, regardless of their specific titles, need to join the war against spying, especially since they are the most vulnerable targets.

How can you join the war against spying? What can you do? What could happen if you don't do anything? *Who's Stealing Your Business?* has been created to answer these questions. But first, let me introduce myself and give you some idea of the path that led me to write this book.

After leaving military service, I became supervisor of investigations for Pinkerton's Inc., in San Francisco. My mentor during the management training program was a senior investigator close to retirement, a fascinating man who was raised in a large prison where his father was the warden. My mentor was a tough little kid who grew up to be a tough investigator with special insights into how criminals think and how crime actually works. This knowledge, plus his talents as a teacher, made him the single biggest inspiration in my career. He helped me realize how honest most people are, and how easily their basic honesty can blind them to the dishonesty lurking close by as they go about their daily tasks. He made sure I wasn't blind, and his tutoring gave me most of my "street smarts."

At that time, Pinkerton's had worked for "450 of the *Fortune 500*," according to Pinkerton's home office in New York City (zip code 10007!). While I was with Pinkerton's, I hired and trained hundreds of security personnel—ninety men and women for one assignment alone. I solicited new business, conferred with clients, planned and staffed operations, and managed all major investigations in the San Francisco office. I frequently had a dozen multi-faceted undercover operations going at the same time.

I became an investigator for the Administrative Services Division of Washington State after leaving Pinkerton's, and conducted financial investigations for several years as part of a pilot program funded by the federal government. We traced assets and people all over the world in an attempt to collect large sums of money owed to the government. I worked closely with elected officials and business leaders to help set up and maintain the program, and I also helped prepare financial recovery cases that were argued in court or at administrative hearings. This program was almost entirely business-oriented and led to the formation of The Questor Group.

The Questor Group is a private consulting firm specializing in business espionage controls and countermeasures. My business partner, Jana Pobiarzyn, is an accountant and former chief financial officer for several companies in Seattle, San Francisco, and Chicago. One of the strengths of The Questor Group is that the people in it have been associated with a very broad range of businesses over the years. The overview it provides is especially useful to clients and to the business managers and executives who read this book.

I've already mentioned a few of the more highly publicized business espionage cases in recent years. Let me now draw from my own experience, and that of my associates in The Questor Group, and describe some cases of business espionage that are a bit more personal and typical. These examples reveal how corporate spying can enter the life of any man or woman who holds citizenship in the business world. I'll begin with a composite case that takes place *outside* the business environment itself. This is the arena where business espionage victims are most likely to be hit, partially because they think they are safer there.

Case History 1: Patent Pending

A patent is poor protection. An investigative reporter once called the entire U.S. patent process "a sham that throws the innovator to the wolves." An attorney interviewed on the subject was much less subtle:

> You had better have a complete marketing program already in the works when you file a patent or you'll lose your ass! The minute you file the papers, some patent attorney or other expert hired by the competition will go over your drawings and specifications with a microscope. If they can find a workable variation of your idea, they may beat you to the marketplace.

Nick may have been thinking along these lines as he drove from his office in Manhattan to his home in upstate New York. Locked in the trunk of his car were his personal computer and the latest version of an important company marketing plan on floppy diskettes. He knew he should keep these materials safe; what he didn't know was that his car had been "modified" in the parking garage that afternoon. There was no major change—an ounce or two of new equipment here and there and a strip of reflective tape. The whole procedure had taken less than a minute and had cost less than $50 in parts.

Halfway home, Nick stopped for a drink as he always did. Leg Man, a business spy, followed Nick into the bar. His partner, Wheel Man, was the one who had modified Nick's car by adding a beeper so that he and Leg Man could stay well back in traffic with the surveillance vehicle and still keep in touch. The tape that Wheel Man had placed unobtrusively above the back window of Nick's car was simply nighttime insurance that the car would be distinguishable.

Leg Man sat down next to Nick in the bar. His job was to

keep his eye on Nick and to start a conversation if the opportunity presented itself. ("Roping," or getting close to a subject without revealing one's motives, is Leg Man's specialty.) Meanwhile, Wheel Man began to burglarize Nick's car. Each spy had a small walkie-talkie in his pocket: One device would produce faint warning clicks when the other device was pressed.

Wheel Man first slipped a flat metal tool between the glass and the gasket of the passenger seat window and lifted the lock latch inside the door. Once inside the car, he pulled the trunk lid open, then scurried back to the trunk and removed the computer and the disks.

If Leg Man had signaled "double for trouble" at this point and Nick had come strolling out of the bar, the whole incident would have looked like a routine theft. Fortunately for the spies, this didn't happen. Stolen information is much more valuable if the victim does not know it has been stolen. Wheel Man copied the floppies on his own equipment. When he was finished, he began to put everything back. At this point, he *did* hear the signal clicks and quickly hid in some nearby bushes.

Nick and Leg Man emerged from the bar laughing—until Nick saw his car. Wheel Man's subsequent report to his client described the event as follows:

> At 7:35 P.M. the subject came out of the Halfway Bar with Agent Leg Man. They had been chatting inside until the subject looked at his watch and got up to leave. Leg Man left with him. When the subject spotted his partially open trunk, he was upset, but then he became relieved when he found that nothing was missing.
>
> When the subject mentioned reporting the matter to the police, Leg Man reminded him that he had been drinking and that this might not look so good to the police or to his boss if the police report became known. The subject initially scoffed at this idea, protesting that he had drunk less than he actually had, but eventually he agreed not to report the break-in. Leg Man is now perceived as a drinking buddy and coconspirator in covering up the crime, so further contact may be relatively easy. It is also useful to know that the subject lies to himself about his drinking.

Here is Wheel Man's report about what happened later that evening:

At 8:47 P.M. the subject arrived at 24 North Road in Keypoksee, where he lives with his wife and teenage son. I maintained my surveillance position until the residence lights went out at 12:26 A.M. and for one hour thereafter. I observed, videotaped, and recorded a number of things that might be useful.

The subject's house is a large, two-story colonial. It sits back from the street on a landscaped lot that provides some privacy but little or no security. There are no outside bells or other indications of a professionally installed burglar alarm, even though alarm warning stickers are posted in all of the downstairs windows. There are no "BLOCK WATCH" signs or other indications of involvement in a neighborhood security program. Most of the neighbors are probably gone during the day.

The subject's house is easy to see into. Most likely, he never walked around the neighborhood and looked back toward his house with that in mind. A wooded area only a block away offers an ideal vantage point for both day and night observations with the proper equipment.

The kitchen and large dining room at the back of the house are mostly glass. Family members post their schedules on the kitchen bulletin board and leave notes to one another and to the cleaning woman. I have their schedules through the end of the week!

During the day the neighborhood is open to any type of service occupation pretext: meter reader, repairperson, pool manufacturer giving free estimates, chimney sweep giving free inspections.

One of the upstairs bedrooms has been remodeled into a private office for the subject. He uses a desktop computer and a Hayes modem attached to the telephone lines. The laptop computer in his car is apparently only a backup. I noted that the modem had been left plugged in for the day and that the computer was on standby to take messages. The computer has a removable hard-disk system, probably to give it the added memory the subject needs to do complete what-if business projections. He apparently doesn't bother to unplug the system or remove the disk when he is away.

We may be able to access whatever he leaves on his computer simply by dialing in and downloading onto our own equipment over the telephone lines. If not, we can tap the telephone lines to get the computer data or use standard bugs to pick up voice communications, or do both. The subject must access the big computer at the company, since he has a shelf of communications manuals above his desk. The titles show on the videotape, so we can check this out.

Because the office is on the second floor, a "spike mike" or other bug will have greater transmitting range. I noted that a tree service has been pruning trees in the neighborhood. An agent with a ladder could pose as a pruner and plant a spike mike high on the side of the house without arousing suspicion. There is also a trellis attached to the back of the house that looks strong enough to climb within reach of the telephone lines.

Poor Nick! Apparently, business spies can now have access to any business documents he works with at home, to any business conversations he initiates or receives at home, and maybe even to his company's mainframe computer. In addition, Nick may have a serious drinking problem that can be exploited: Perhaps this is why he has to take work home with him. His boss may not even know that highly important materials are leaving the office!

This case is not meant to suggest that the office environment is much more secure from business espionage than is the home. Espionage can also rear its ugly head in an office setting.

Case History 2: The Peephole Perplexity

Linda is a middle-level public relations executive for a company with offices in a modern building. There are rental stores on the ground floor and other tenants on other floors, including her own. Linda especially likes the fact that her office has a private entrance to the hallway leading past the elevators, even though she shares this hallway with strangers from other firms.

Linda sometimes stays late in the office, catching up on her paperwork while the rush-hour traffic thins out. She has a lot of business acumen. Like most of her peers, however, she knew little about security until she was forced to face the possibility that her personal privacy was being invaded. Up to that time, the only *thoughts she had about security revolved around her home and her two teenage children, who were sometimes left alone in the evenings.*

When Linda voiced her worries about her children's safety, a friend told her about a new subminiature TV camera system that can be mounted behind a front-door peephole. The homeowner can then see if a stranger is lurking anywhere outside before opening the door. Intrigued by the concept of a TV camera and monitor that could fit inside her purse, Linda researched other security gear and discovered systems that could print photographs of what the TV saw and/or send the TV picture over telephone lines, all by remote control. She also learned that business spies bought and used a major share of this equipment, so she began to look around her office with new eyes. Here is her story in her own words:

> I was locking up my office after working late one Friday and I started thinking again about a peephole security camera for my front door at home. I turned around and noticed a funny mark on the door of an office at the end of the hall. I examined this mark closely and, sure enough, it looked like a peephole!
>
> At first, I couldn't believe that what I saw was a peephole; I thought I was just being paranoid. I knew the door led to a storeroom, but it wasn't a storeroom for my company, so I couldn't get inside to inspect things. Instead, I called building security. The man I talked to said that security didn't use miniature cameras—only full-size ones in plain view in the lobby and parking garage. He said he would report my finding to building management.
>
> In the meantime, I asked some of my business associates if they had ever run across any spy-related activities in their jobs. I was shocked at how many of them had a story to tell!
>
> One woman I spoke with heads the communications department of a large newspaper. She found out after the fact that she was under constant surveillance by her boss, who suspected there was a leak in her department. She was even being watched during lunch hour when she was off the premises.
>
> Another acquaintance of mine, a production automation specialist, answered a blind help-wanted ad to a post office box, sending his résumé and a description of the types of projects he handled. When he didn't get a reply, he just forgot about it. The ad turned out to be a phony placed by a competitor. When the competitor realized that my friend's work was

of interest to him, the competitor hired a private eye to do what he called a "background investigation on a prospective employee." The operation was nothing more than a spy campaign masquerading as a fairly common and quasi-legal business practice.

In time, Linda noticed that the peephole on the storeroom door down the hall had disappeared. When she checked with security, she learned that a camera and recorder system had been discovered and removed, but that the spy or spies behind the system had not been identified. A great number of customers, sales reps, and media people go in and out of Linda's office. A law firm down the hall also sees a lot of traffic. In sum, the hallway is crossed by numerous possible spies or spy victims who could account for the presence of a hidden camera. Linda was baffled: Had a crime been committed or not?

ETHICAL VS. UNETHICAL RESEARCH

As these examples of business espionage show, it is not easy to draw a firm line between what can definitely be called spying and what might more properly be called sharp intelligence gathering. The problem gets even trickier with the added issue of legal vs. illegal conduct. Each incident must be judged on its own, and frequently the only criterion for passing judgment is whether the episode as a whole strikes the individual observer (who could be the potential perpetrator, the actual victim, or the judge in court) as moral or immoral.

The best approach I can take in this book is to communicate my own beliefs regarding which types of business research conduct are ethical and which types are not. Since most experts seem to agree with my judgments, I'm confident that they are worth offering.

The Ethical Top Ten

1. *Listening.* It is perfectly ethical to keep your ears open at all times. In fact, the number one source of information is the person who talks too much. A successful spy is a good listener, and an honest businessperson should be equally good, if not better. Staying alert to everything that goes on in the workplace makes sound moral sense for anyone!

2. *Using computer data banks, published materials, court records, and similar sources open to the public.* It is almost always ethical to use such information, even when the competition gives away more than it intended. A personal computer can, for example, sort through hundreds of trade journals, magazines, and newspapers for references to the XYZ Company in a matter of minutes. These data can be updated automatically by placing a standing order with a local computer service.

3. *Attending seminars, exhibits, and trade fairs.* All of these are good sources of business information and are also arenas where some degree of digging and snooping is common and even expected. Though it is possible to go too far, normally these events are fair game.

4. *Debriefing the sales force and others in the field.* Regular interviews with your personnel who have frequent customer contact can provide valuable information on competitors. Service technicians, for example, often know exactly who is installing what, and where. In the course of one undercover assignment for a client, I often met sales reps from other companies for coffee and friendly conversation at a local diner. When I told my client this, he went to his salespeople for some inside information—and got lots of it. Asked why he hadn't come forward with such information before, one sales rep replied, "You never asked!"

5. *Performing reverse engineering, or analysis of the competitors' products or services.* This practice is usually deemed ethical, providing the product or service is in the public domain. A company that works on other products as well as its own is automatically in the business of reverse engineering. I suspect that certain repair facilities are set up for this very purpose!

6. *Conducting market surveys.* Survey information is vital to the business world and can be used in many ways. What-if scenarios on the computer can sort data gathered by others and break it down to fit a company's specific needs.

7. *Seeking outside experts.* Consultants can provide critical industry overviews and are in most cases legitimate—they have to

be to survive! When hiring consultants, be sure to check their credentials carefully.

8. *Studying financial reports and research documents released by competitors.* Time spent brainstorming these materials with company financial officers as well as with outside experts can be invaluable. Simply ask, "How would *we* get these figures if *we* were doing it?" The answer will often reveal how a competitor got them and, therefore, what they mean.

9. *Gaining information from legitimate employment interviews with employees of competitors.* This practice is often quite useful, and a company is free to ask any questions, providing the employee came there voluntarily.

10. *Using headhunters as a source of inside information.* When headhunters attempt to place people, they may inadvertently reveal information about other companies. Any company is free to probe in this regard—as long as it is careful about what it reveals in return. Media people often use headhunters in employment agencies and placement services as important sources of confidential business information. One business reporter claims that her headhunter contacts give her many of her best leads.

The Dirty Dozen

1. *Trespassing on property owned by a competitor.* This practice is always unethical.

2. *Secretly observing someone's activities or property.* Covert action is the essence of what is meant by spying. One business executive routinely walks through the parking lot at a business park and looks into the cars of competitors. He doesn't bug the cars or even touch them; he just looks at everything exposed to view: samples, clipboards, letters, even bumper stickers. He claims to learn a great deal about the competition this way!

3. *Using electronic eavesdropping equipment.* Bugging someone's territory with a listening or viewing device is morally offensive and usually illegal.

4. *Learning trade secrets by hiring people who work for a competitor.* Using hired spies, whether they continue to work for the competition or leave and come to work for the company, is definitely unethical.

In the latter case, what the spies are doing may be illegal, and a company may become implicated in a court suit as an abettor. Employees who may be privy to important trade secrets are usually required to sign a nondisclosure agreement at the time they are hired. The agreement legally prohibits them from sharing information with a competitor if and when they leave. Some agreements even bar employees from taking a job with a competitor for a specified time after they leave.

5. *Hiring a spy (or a professional investigator) to get specific information from another company.* Most people would consider this practice unethical, whether or not it is legal. Naturally, it is *not* unethical to hire a private investigator to uncover thieves in the company, make background checks, or protect employees and company property.

6. *Placing an undercover agent employee on a competitor's payroll.* This practice is always unethical.

7. *Stealing documents or property, even if the stolen items are later replaced.* Stealing is both unethical and illegal.

8. *Conducting phony negotiations for a license, a franchise, or a distributorship in order to gain inside information.* Such deceptive practices are always unethical.

9. *Gaining information by staging a market research study or similar interview project.* Any action undertaken under false pretenses is unethical.

10. *Bribing.* Any form of bribery is unethical and, possibly, illegal.

11. *Blackmailing.* Any form of blackmail is unethical and, possibly, illegal.

12. *Extorting.* Any form of extortion is unethical and, possibly, illegal.

FALCONS AND PIGEONS

One reason it is difficult to pin guilt on business spies is that their victims so often leave themselves wide open to espionage efforts. In other words, they invite and assist the spying! Here is a true story that also serves as a parable for the "What me, guilty?" dilemma.

Binoculars and telescopes sit on the windowsills and balconies of countless office buildings. They can be found in New York City and in small-town America. Occasionally a balcony will even feature a Questar telescope that can read and photograph almost anything—from the license plates of cars a mile away to valuable papers left on someone's desk.

A company's executive offices are usually located in the front of the building, with key personnel situated in corner offices that offer wide-angle views, both for people looking out and for people looking in. Many meetings held in these offices feature large graphs, chalkboards, and oversized blueprints that are easy to see and interpret for those sitting far away—maybe even a mile away with a little mechanical help.

A controls and countermeasures specialist once walked in on a man who was using a telescope to view nearby office buildings. He asked the man what he was looking for. "Peregrine falcons," the man replied. "The falcons have come back to the city to nest on the ledges and hunt the pigeons. But I don't have to tell you anything. Telescopes aren't illegal. What's it to you?"

What, indeed, could it be to anyone? It's impossible to prove that someone is spying in a case like this. True, the peregrine *is* back in many cities. True, too, a well-publicized espionage case, later popularized in Robert Lindsay's best-selling book *The Falcon and the Snowman* (New York: Simon & Schuster, 1980), has made "falcon" the new buzzword for spy.

"Pigeons" abound in any office environment. Some pigeons do not draw the drapes during important meetings. Others do not safeguard valuable papers, shield their computer screens, consider the environment around them when they are doing important work, or follow any of the basic security precautions to protect themselves.

Prevention is the best espionage control and countermeasure for any business, no matter how big or small. No activity is exempt from danger; no career is safe. The chapters ahead identify the falcons in business espionage and the ways to avoid becoming a pigeon.

CHAPTER 2

Who's at Risk, What's at Risk:

The Industries and Information That Spies Target

> *"The present world can be designated as one of business and war."*
> **Yukichi Fukuzawa, samurai founder of Keio University**

One of the world's most valuable business secrets—the formula for Merchandise 7X—rests under twenty-four-hour guard in a basement vault of Atlanta's Trust Company Bank. So stringently does Coca-Cola protect its century-old recipe for Classic Coke (aka Merchandise 7X) that only two executives know its contents, and their contracts prohibit them from flying on the same plane. In 1985, Coca-Cola's lawyers defied a federal court order to share the precious formula with Classic Coke's major bottlers, even though the information would have helped the bottlers to price syrups and, ultimately, to produce a more cost-effective product. According to the lawyers' statement, "The formula might become public and, if it did, cause incalculable and irreparable harm to the company." ("Businesses Struggle to Keep Their Secrets," *U.S. News & World Report,* September 23, 1985.)

Major corporations are not the only ones with secrets to keep. Every business must develop a competitive edge to survive. And it isn't just special formulas that are at risk. In the eyes of rival companies, any information about how an organization operates, or intends to operate, is potentially desirable. Dishonest rivals may steal or pay for:

- Details of a company's material costs, contract bids, sales statistics, profit margins, or financial projections.
- Outlines of research findings, new product ideas, promotional strategies, or announcement dates.
- Lists of customers, suppliers, work schedules, or organizational project assignments.
- Specifications on a company's workplace, plant capacities, or expansion plans.

Much of this information is impossible to hide under lock and key. It needs to circulate from person to person, from department to department, and from city to city in order for a business to function properly.

More to the point, it's difficult to identify the particular scraps of data that may be useful to an outsider—or to an insider who can sell it to an outsider. A routing list on a memo about a customer service proposal may contain the very names a competitor needs to start investigating a company's future marketing strategy, or to complete the picture it has been covertly assembling for some time. Pieces of personal, corporate, and scientific data that seem trivial in themselves can become crucial when combined with other information through data processing.

For an unscrupulous management, spying is smart business— a way to get million-dollar data at bargain basement prices. And business is war. By using spies, a company gains the satisfaction not only of saving a great deal of cost, time, and effort but also of netting information that may be critical to a rival's success or failure.

Corporate espionage has always been a major problem in high-technology companies, where fortunes ride on intricately detailed (and documented) advances in technological design. In a highly publicized spying case in June 1982, seventeen Japanese business executives, mainly from Hitachi and Mitsubishi, were charged with paying an undercover FBI agent over $600,000 to steal structural blueprints and software codes for IBM's mainframe computer. Their subsequent confession sparked a scandal in Japan and led to the abrupt resignation of several top executives.

The scope of industrial espionage is broadening rapidly. Increasing numbers of low-tech companies are rushing to embrace new technology while cutting expenses. Most of them, little aware of industrial espionage and unable to assess espionage risks with any accuracy, lack explicit policies, procedures, or guidelines to guard against corporate spying. In many respects, these companies are more easily victimized than the larger, more technological organizations, which are accustomed to being alert.

THE HILLENBRAND SAGA

Hillenbrand Industries, a casket manufacturer based in Batesville, Indiana, is a case in point. Although Hillenbrand holds its own in a relatively stagnant market, other casket makers are consolidating into formidable opposition, and the entire industry is facing rapid advances in metals coating and factory automation. What happened at Hillenbrand over three years of escalating competition illustrates not only the wide range of information a corporate spy may find attractive but also the dangerously corrosive effect a single career of business espionage can have—putting everyone and everything in its path at risk.

The story begins in May 1984, when Marc Feith, a highly regarded financial analyst for Hillenbrand, started receiving periodic assignments from management to gather intelligence on material and labor costs, production volume, and future plans from competitors and potential acquisition targets.

First on Feith's list was Amedco Inc., a competitor based in St. Louis. Just before dawn one morning, Feith raided a trash dumpster at the company's steel division in Springfield, Missouri, and unexpectedly struck gold. "I found complete information on what Amedco was paying for steel for its caskets," Feith said later, "and it was less than we were paying. That discovery helped Hillenbrand renegotiate steel prices and save nearly $3 million a year." He also pieced together valuable information on cash flow and operations, as well as advance notice about Amedco's plans to merge with Service Corporation.

Although Hillenbrand executives deny that they were aware of Feith's tactics, his information apparently whetted their appetites for more. A Hillenbrand memo dated December 10, 1985, reveals that Feith was assigned to create ("if possible") a cost summary of fourteen competitors, including information on "average hourly production rate, plant capacity, shipping methods, and collective bargaining agreements."

Pursuing these data at the offices of Aurora Casket Company, Feith paid a trash hauler $100 on one occasion and $50 on another to let him search the truck. The third time, the hauler refused. "He wondered how he would explain it if I got crushed in the compactor," Feith recalled. So Feith rented a truck, followed the trash hauler to the dump, and collected the papers that were dropped there.

In February 1986, Hillenbrand decided to slow down its acquisition plans and no longer sought Feith's type of information. He was reassigned. One executive, mindful of Feith's discontent over shrinking advancement opportunities, advised him to look for a job outside the company.

Disappointment and resentment took their toll over the next few months. Feith had put up with strange hours and the risk of getting caught. He had overcome his initial distaste for spying in the belief that the results would greatly benefit his company as well as his career. "At Hillenbrand," Feith once claimed, "the company's attitude is simple: The only good competitor is a dead competitor." Now Feith feared that all his hard work would come to nothing, for both himself and Hillenbrand.

Feith decided to reenter the war, except that this time he would get even: He would betray Hillenbrand. Over several days in late April 1986, he burrowed into company files and made copies of corporate revenue forecasts and such research secrets as Hillenbrand's new epoxy sealing formula. Altogether he copied about 5,000 pages of documents, which he collated into twenty-two hardbound volumes, indexed by a four-page catalog of prices totaling $106,000.

Identifying himself as "Clark Kent," Feith approached B. D. Hunter, vice-president of Service Corporation, and said, "I have your competitor's five-year plans." Hunter stalled negotiations and alerted the FBI. Feith was eventually arrested.

In October 1987, after a two-week trial, U.S. District Judge Sarah Evans Baker sentenced Feith to sixty days in jail and a $3,000 fine. Although she refused to allow information on Feith's spying for Hillenbrand as a defense, she did scold Hillenbrand management. "I won't put my stamp of approval on what may have gone on down there," she said, urging Hillenbrand to get its house in order.

Today, thanks to Feith's exposure, the casket industry is far more alert to the possibility of espionage. "We have shredders now, and we changed janitorial services," Hunter comments. "Of course, we still wonder if some of our employees are actually Hillenbrand's." David Gooch, Service Corporation's attorney, promises, "We'll sue Hillenbrand if we ever find out that other information they took from our trash is being used to hurt us."

The Hillenbrand case is a classic illustration of how espionage can thrive for years—undetected and unchecked—within any business community. It's human nature to balk at imagining what trouble *could* happen. Most people simply dodge the issue by saying, "I don't want to get paranoid" or "The chances of anything disastrous happening are too small to worry about." It's not pleasant to conjure up images of who or what is at risk in an organization. Not unless you're a spy for the competition!

That's exactly the game you must play to gain a worthwhile perspective on the threat of espionage: Imagine you are a spy and explore every facet of your organization—its personnel, procedures, records, products, contacts, and physical plant—to ferret out weaknesses. A possibility that seems farfetched or insignificant to you may not be to a diligent, talented, and well-paid sleuth.

Here's a look at various types of businesses and the potentially unimaginable—yet real—espionage targets they represent to interested parties.

RESEARCH COMPANIES AT RISK

Because a new idea or product is an invaluable prize in any industry, research centers are particularly attractive locales for corporate espionage. They are also highly vulnerable. Research projects typically generate mountains of data that circulate among a wide assortment of highly individualistic workers: full-time specialists, contract employees or part-time staff, and freelance consultants and other semi-independent agents with tenuous organizational loyalties. The odds that some important pieces of information will fall into the wrong hands are very high.

No research can be considered safe, whether it takes place in a guarded, multistory lab facility closed to the outside world or on a chemist's workbench in a small shop with virtually unlimited public access. Today, large firms so often farm things out to contractors that the smaller outfit may be where the research war is actually won or lost.

In one chemicals plant, the senior chemist was working on the formula for a new product. He sat at a bench near a window with a nice view of a landscaped parking area. A nice view out is a nice view in. A trusted colleague proved to be a spy who haunted the parking area, peeked through the window, and did everything but count the jojoba seeds that went into the new formula.

The battle to be first, or best, or most profitable often inspires spy commandos to come up with amazingly ingenious strategies. Walking through a parking lot, for example, a spy may take note of the various types of parking stickers on research employees' cars. Parking stickers tell a lot about the status and activities of the driver, both at the target facility and anywhere else the person has parking privileges. A sticker showing that a targeted employee parks near a campus research center may provide valuable clues about that worker's special education and responsibilities and activities away from the job.

A "spook" once traced a research assistant to a campus where she was doing graduate work at night. The spy bought some of the researcher's used books and "borrowed" others. The yellow highlighting pen that the researcher used while reading the books turned out to be a valuable indicator of activities back in the target company's research lab.

Office politics, suppression of research, sabotage of experiments, squabbles over authorship, and rebellion among experts are problems that plague any research program. Business espionage can cause these problems, or make them worse, or take advantage of them.

MANUFACTURING COMPANIES AT RISK

It is no accident that most media stories of business espionage involve manufacturing firms. Tangible products—and the dynamic processes that go into making them—not only possess high visual impact in themselves but also fascinate an insatiably curious consumer audience. In 1986, news broadcasters and reporters had a field day when they discovered that Soviet "business executives" touring a Boeing aircraft plant wore crepe-soled shoes to pick up metal shavings and other debris for later analysis. Out from the news files poured a flood of similar incidents featuring "pickup" boxes with hinged bottoms and briefcases with sticky tape on the underside.

The vulnerability of a manufacturing company is not limited to its production line. As one divisional manager at a vehicle manufacturing plant put it, "We do it all: research, development, purchasing, assembly, and sales. Our neck is stuck out in every direction at once."

This manager was wise to be so concerned. His plant assembles very expensive cars, vans, and trucks built to the customer's specifications. He knew that his unique methods of operation and custom-designed materials presented highly attractive targets. Sure enough, undercover agents hired by the company found information leaks, outright thefts of major vehicle components, and even acts of sabotage.

An employee who had faked his background to cover a jail record for theft was stealing company documents and passing them on to someone he had met in prison: The two men hoped to take over some of the company's business for themselves. The employee's job as a parts runner gave him access to most areas within the plant. All he had to do was follow the paper trail and track down missing parts and accessories.

As the in-house thief later confessed, he acquired a lot more than just parts and accessories. He swiped blank company routing slips ("so we could get what we wanted by ordering direct from the other departments"), lists of vehicle customers ("so we could sell them accessories"), and operations manuals ("so we'd know what was going on and how to get around it").

Investigators found a stockpile of stolen vehicle parts in a barn on a nearby island. The smaller parts were shipped directly to the thieves by means of pilfered routing slips. The larger, heavier parts were stolen by forklift and hoisted over the company fence. The smaller items were in the $50-to-$100 range. The larger items were worth several thousand dollars apiece!

One of the undercover agents, also a parts runner, observed numerous acts of sabotage committed by fellow employees who felt they were worked too hard and paid too little—a common complaint, whether justified or not, at plants specializing in luxury goods. Most of the unrest was caused by a small group of malcontents who preached such get-even tactics as rerouting needed materials, mixing up paperwork to cover thefts, and bending vehicle components out of alignment. When managers became aware of the problem, they redesigned the routing slips so that they could tell at a glance who ordered a part, who took it from stock, who "ran" it, and who received it.

This vehicle manufacturing plant also conducted practical research—informal experimentation outside of research departments, "where the wheel hits the road." In this situation, the spy's payoff is quicker because the target product is already in use. Undercover investigators at the plant monitored some practical research on a short section of the production line. Tests were being run on a new fiberglass molding process that would speed up a rather slow and labor-intensive part of the overall manufacturing operation.

Employees involved in the tests were more concerned about how the new processes would affect their jobs than about streamlining production for the company. One molder complained to his co-workers, "If we push this process through, it will cut our overtime." Even the automation engineer in charge of the tests was upset about the progress: "I don't want to go back to the technical pool any sooner than I have to." A little undercover digging revealed that the engineer was looking for another position, and was carrying what he knew about his present employer into the marketplace with him.

When the division manager who initiated the investigation saw the report about these "short line" workers, he redefined their jobs to make them more closely allied to the research team itself. He fired the traitorous engineer and put the best of the other employees on a competitive bonus system as "production specialists." There is now more emphasis on extra money for innovation rather than for overtime. In his campaign to make his area of responsibility more secure, the manager also gained a more efficient and harmonious workforce.

TRANSPORTATION COMPANIES AT RISK

Without a doubt, transportation is one of the industries most susceptible to business espionage. Ironically, it is also an industry that is highly neglectful in countering espionage. Transportation involves so much activity spread over so much territory that it is fiendishly difficult to create a tight system of security checks and controls. Moreover, individual acts of espionage are usually aimed at the clients of a transportation company, not the company itself, so management is not strongly motivated to take an aggressive approach to security.

The bottom line is this: Every organization that uses a transportation company must analyze and actively combat the business espionage risks inherent in transportation.

Information changes hands each time a product does. Shipping orders, invoices, and bills of lading all tell part of the story. So does each piece of supporting documentation, in house or out. A company may set up excellent security measures on its own turf but find that what it considers confidential information is just another piece of paper to the outfit moving its products. For example, many firms consider the number of product units sold each month to be classified information. Yet a shipping order for 26,000 cardboard containers of a certain size and shape, inscribed with the company logo and unit description, may be sitting on the loading dock of a transportation company for all to see.

Indirect sources of production data abound in the industry. One manufacturer that bought keyboards from outside discovered that a transporter's records of the number of keyboards shipped in revealed the number of computers the company would soon be shipping out. In another case involving a newspaper publisher, the number of Sunday supplements that were printed by an outside firm revealed the paper's Sunday circulation.

A spy who locates a company's source of supply and delivery may be able to determine that company's production capacity, sales volume, customers, and more. Company managers interested in locating spies—or spiable information—must cooperate actively with transportation executives to ensure that confidential information stays confidential.

UTILITY COMPANIES AT RISK

Utility companies are particularly vulnerable to espionage because their "product" must often travel long distances through areas with little built-in security. Anyone who knows what's happening along this extended line of service can easily cause trouble.

The manager of an electric power company in the Southwest suspected that a security leak lay behind robberies that had cost his company thousands of dollars in lost property and wasted time. The company was stringing lines in remote desert areas as part of a maintenance and expansion program. Workers would quit for the day and return the next morning to find their equipment gone. Even huge rolls of wire would disappear. The situation got so bad that workers had to bring all their equipment—even the big, slow-moving trailers—back to base camp at the end of each day. This procedure wasted an enormous amount of time and labor.

The utility manager thought it was more than a coincidence that the thieves always seemed to know exactly where the crews were operating in a territory he described as "miles and miles of nothing but miles and miles." Working closely with security consultants, he discovered that a clerk at company headquarters was passing along copies of the line crew schedules to a friend who knew someone in the salvage business.

The theft of copper wire and other metals is such a problem in this region, as in many underpopulated areas, that local police and sheriff's departments often employ a full-time "salvage detective." Since this particular problem came under the jurisdiction of a salvage detective, the evidence was handed over to the authorities, who later obtained convictions of two of the people involved.

Sabotage is another special risk utility companies face. A former official of the Burns International Security Service once handled "the case of the disgruntled ratepayer." The customer used a labor dispute as a cover for blowing up a power station, executing his crime during strike negotiations at the utility company. An outsider, the saboteur apparently obtained information about the stations by breaking into maintenance vehicles and stealing maps and manuals. Since other items were also missing, the drivers of these vehicles would naturally consider the break-ins to be simple burglaries.

Utility companies, of course, are also frequently abused by customers who just want to wriggle out of paying their bills. A fellow private investigator, I am sorry to say, used information from a California utility company to outwit its master computer. He ran up utility bills at his apartment and then sent what looked like normal change-of-address information through the utility company computer with the help of a woman friend who worked there as a computer input supervisor. He didn't actually move; he just closed out one utility account and opened another one under a phony name. Since utility companies routinely check out these changes, the plan wouldn't have worked without the help of his friend.

One day I made an unexpected visit to this investigator's apartment to pick up a last-minute report. His friend was with him. As he was completing the report, she told me all about how the scam worked, thinking I would want to get in on it. It turned out they were passing on their methods to a large number of people, including a sizable group at a local university. Some of the information even got into the underground press!

When one of the people who learned of the scam turned the crooked operator in, the utility company came after him, and he finally fled. The utility was left with a substantial loss of revenue—and a die-hard suspicion of undercover agents. Still, the company does continue to employ agents as necessary contributors to its intensified security program. Private investigators are carefully regulated in California. As in all the professions, a bad one some-times slips through. (Chapter 7 examines how to "qualify" and oversee outside security agents to avoid such a problem.)

SERVICE COMPANIES AT RISK

Service organizations live on information. It is safe to say that information is a major portion of their inventory. Often, mailing lists and lists of business contacts are primarily what a buyer is paying for when a service company changes hands. Such lists are certainly what a dishonest competitor pays a spy to deliver.

A typical service company employs lots of skilled, part-time labor: people who are clever, technologically literate, and frequently desperate to find satisfying, full-time employment. One service company hired just such a temporary worker to put its mailing list onto its new computer system. The worker downloaded a copy of the list onto spare disks and used these disks in her personal job hunt. First, she composed a matrix letter on her personal computer; then she merged the mailing list with the letter to customize her job search. It's a common practice—and a common ripoff of information that should be kept strictly confidential.

Customer data entries in "mail merging" and similar software programs usually begin with seven basic items: the entry number, the person's title, the company's name, the company's street address, the rest of the company's address, the person's name without the title, and the company's regional location. Of course, most company data files contain more than just the seven basics. Each service company decides for itself what is important, and its computer filing system may include dozens of other vital bits and pieces of information for each entry that can be broken down in a number of ways to accomplish a number of purposes.

For example, using a personal computer, the part-time service employee could easily have broken down the stolen list by zip codes to isolate desirable working locations. Depending on how the list was organized, she might have gone one step further and skimmed the list according to a "best customer" code in order to start her own competitive firm. The uses of a copied mailing list are limited only by the thief's imagination and ability to operate a computer.

- A spy can do a custom mailing on a computer-designed letterhead as a "research project" to gauge the potential market for a new service or service organization. A computer-generated survey sheet could be part of the package. This kind of customized "desktop printing" is becoming more and more common.

- A spy can take advantage of coded lists that show how much a customer buys and how much that customer pays for a direct mail campaign offering a special service or incentive.

- A spy can sort out Mr., Mrs., and Ms. designations as well as corporate titles to focus on a specific, profitable portion of the market.

A stolen data file can offer an outsider precious insight into the strengths and weaknesses of a company. This is especially true in service companies, where success depends heavily on the manipulation of statistical and demographic information. Service company managers need to be especially sensitive to the fact that mailing lists, client records, and contact files are maps in the war of business espionage.

My associates and I at Questor have a professional stake in not being alarmists. But experience tells us that no one in business is completely safe from espionage. Recently I hosted a seminar discussion group on corporate spying. One businessman commented that his company had never had a substantial business loss, that most people were honest, and that the whole espionage problem was overblown. I interrupted him before he could name his company. I didn't want to be responsible for pointing a company out as a potential easy mark, with managers who didn't think the espionage problem existed.

WHAT DO SPIES STEAL?

"Start where you are now" is the best approach to business espionage controls and countermeasures. Viewing spying from that perspective first requires a look at what spies are after. The primary target in business espionage is information. How companies gather and use information determines to a large extent who will be first, best, or most profitable in an honest marketplace. Dishonest operatives and their clients also want to be first, best, and most profitable, but at the expense of others. For these reasons, the "start where you are now" approach focuses on a personal survey of the information at hand. Every manager in every organization should ask: "What company information exists within my area of responsibility? How might that information be attractive to a spy? How might I prevent a spy from getting it?" To answer these questions effectively, the manager must think as a corporate spy would think.

Spies Steal Ideas

The head of the special products division at a steel mill asked a team of agents to work undercover while he was implementing plans to modify an automatic torch so that it would cut steel plate in new and intricate designs. His caution was well advised. One of the machinists had been leaking this information to a relative in another company. The rival company manufactured an entirely different metal product but used the same cutting technology. Because of the dissimilarity in end products, the theft might have gone unnoticed—except for the tip from the undercover operatives.

Machinists, especially tool and die makers, are a rather close-knit community. They often have part-time jobs on the side and mutual contacts in other companies. Too often there are no company guidelines concerning how these outside contacts should be handled. After the spying episode at the steel mill, the head of the special products division sought advice from outside experts and did some research on his own. Armed with specific recommendations, he made sure that his organization drafted and publicized a very strict set of regulations and penalties relating to disclosure of company information.

Spies Steal Product Information

The special products division at this steel mill constitutes a separate world from the rest of the plant. The general manager's office is a glass box in a huge, hangarlike room. Supervisors, senior machinists, blueprint clerks, and clean-up people come and go freely at all hours. Profit and loss memos, research and development forecasts, and other sensitive papers are in plain view of any visitor, and their contents are often openly discussed in a visitor's presence. As a result, without being officially told, undercover operatives learned where the department ranked in productivity, which new products were expected to be winners and why, plus estimated future production figures.

Following the undercover investigation, the general manager asked outside security consultants for recommendations on how to eliminate security risks. The consultants recommended that some management information be reserved for particular people on a need-to-know basis, but without destroying the family atmosphere that worked so well in other respects. The consultants also helped the manager devise an informal paper-filing system that was just as convenient as the old one but far more private.

Spies Steal Marketing Plans

The steel mill's special products division had two copy machines: one in the general manager's office and another in a cubicle used by the supervisors. One undercover agent watched a fellow employee take a shipping list out of the manager's office and photocopy it on the supervisors' machine. He explained to the agent that the copies were for his own use.

Undercover operatives must often decide whether to report an incident at the time it is happening, and run the risk of attracting attention to themselves, or wait until they write their regular summary. The basic rule is to do what any other honest employee would do, as long as it doesn't jeopardize the cover. This agent decided to act. He asked his supervisor, who did not know an undercover operation was in progress, about company policy on using the copy machines. The supervisor answered, "No problem. Just don't hog the machine. We don't have any hard-and-fast rules on that, but clear it with me about any company stuff. One of the guys has a weekend business doing mop-on roofing for factories and schools. I let him copy the shipping lists to get new customers. It's no big deal, but check with me."

Security consultants later recommended some hard-and-fast rules concerning company documents and the use of copy machines—not because of the employee in the roofing business, but because of others who might be in the spy business. They also suggested a checkout system for materials leaving the manager's office.

Spies Steal Supplier Information

The steel mill has a railroad siding where boxcars are shunted up to the warehouse loading dock during the night and unloaded during the day. As part of their undercover work, agents often sat in their cars during breaks and watched the warehouse crew unload the materials used by the special products division.

The housings for one type of equipment were shipped in from another manufacturer. Agents counted these units to estimate the next production run—and to calculate their own potential overtime as employees. Spies for another firm might have counted them to estimate production. They might also have backtracked to the supplier to get costs and other information. Suppliers are usually much more open about purchase data than the companies they supply. The supplier is always on the lookout for new customers and will sometimes reveal confidential data about one customer in order to get another.

The biggest security problem with the loading dock was that it was completely visible from a cross street. A spy with a video camera could easily tape the entire unloading process. Part of the solution to the problem involved building a simple "privacy panel" at the end of the loading dock. As a result, no matter where the spy parked on the nearby cross street, a video camera could not catch everything going in and out.

Spies Steal Personnel Information

The more a spy knows about the people who work in a company, the better his or her chances of cultivating a contact that will pay off—someone who has an expertise to tap, an interest to share, an ambition to feed, or a weakness to exploit. As obvious as this fact may be, many organizations are surprisingly careless about letting important personnel information circulate.

One in-house newsletter available in a public lobby printed employee identification numbers as a part of a "spot your number and win a prize" contest. In the wrong hands, these numbers could be used to get company information over the telephone or through the computer. If nothing else, an employee's number is probably a key to that employee's personal computer records. Any experienced spy with a list of employee numbers already has one foot in the door of a potentially invaluable room of information.

A disgruntled employee working for a multifaceted corporation based in Seattle stole information from computerized personnel files the day before she left her job. She then sent anonymous letters to people in the corporation detailing policies that allegedly exploited workers who fit their job descriptions. Her efforts caused a storm of controversy. Once she was exposed, the letter recipients realized the irrational foundation of her action.

Spies Steal Information for Counterfeiting

Outright piracy of formulas, designs, and production processes in order to create bogus "original" goods is a constant in the business world. The marketplace abounds with fake versions of Cartier watches, Levi's jeans, Gucci purses, and similar high-quality, brand-name merchandise. Often these sham products look very much like their more costly originals.

Far more common and far more insidious is the theft of a company's "image" to sell a product or service that, in fact, has little or no resemblance to the genuine article. Working at the request of the vice-president of a chemicals plant, a group of undercover operatives discovered that the supervisor of the packaging department had been stealing expensive carnauba wax products in 55-gallon drums for resale to janitorial services and other private customers. When he could no longer get the product itself, the supervisor didn't miss a beat. He simply stole stacks of labels off the automatic labeler on the production line, concocted an inferior product in his garage, and continued selling wax to his established customers and to new ones, despite the fact that his wax didn't look like, or function like, what it claimed to be.

Crooks offering counterfeit services also depend on labels. To enhance a phony sales presentation, the counterfeiter may use actual sales materials purloined from the legitimate firm. One U.S. security guard company even borrowed the name, reputation, and procedural format of a much bigger English firm for several years.

The manager of the counterfeit U.S. concern laughed when he talked about it!

Spies Steal Security Information

I've placed security information last on my list, but most successful spies put it first on their lists. It is shockingly easy for clever employees or infiltrators to learn a great deal about the ways a company protects its physical and intellectual property (that is, business data, plans, and procedures). In a high percentage of espionage-related crimes, a little casual snooping, camouflaged chitchat, and quick outside reference work can give spies all they need to know to get what they want and then get away.

Guard schedules and procedures are often posted on bulletin boards or kept near entrances and exits, where anyone with a mind to can read the information. Employees in charge of sensitive files routinely open locked drawers and doors without giving a thought to who might be watching while they check a written combination, manipulate the lock itself, or replace a key in a poorly secured storage spot. Some companies even keep file cabinets marked SECURITY in heavily trafficked areas.

Unfortunately, many managers feel they've bought security with the installation of an electronic surveillance system. This is certainly a step in the right direction, but it is not a fail-safe solution. After installation, model numbers and components are often in plain view. With these clues, a reasonably intelligent spy can first track down material that will reveal how the system operates, and then figure out how to get around the system.

To reinforce a point made earlier in this chapter: All companies are at risk from outside firms that provide them with essential equipment and services but do not adequately safeguard records. One equipment catalog makes this clear in its effort to promote a do-it-yourself security system:

> Did you know that many alarm installation firms have in their often unlocked filing cabinets not only complete diagrams of the alarm wiring pattern but floor plans that cover crawlspaces, door and window openings, heat and air ducts, ventilation returns, attic ventilators, and so on? These plans may

also diagram so-called secure areas, indicating the exact location of safes, vaults, and other forms of lockboxes. What if such plans were to fall into the wrong hands?

Most electronic security systems—whether purchased or developed in house, or a combination of the two—are primarily effective in thwarting brute entry. Most business spies, however, are not brutes but sophisticated operators. In addition to considering what a spy may want to steal, a manager concerned with uncovering and preventing espionage needs to consider who spies are: Why do people become spies? How are they set up? What are the tricks of their trade? The answers to these questions are detailed in Chapter 3.

The Enemy Among Us:

Spies on Staff
and Undercover Infiltrators

Tafsir il aam [*"Throw away the rule book that keeps you from winning the game"*]
Arab saying

It's 6:30 P.M. and everyone has left the office building except the overnight security personnel. All the drawers, doors, and windows are locked. The electronic alarm system and closed-circuit video monitors are fully operative. Only one stairway and one elevator provide access to the upper floors; in the ground-level lobby, a guard is always seated in full view of the entrances.

It's 9:05 A.M. the following day. A vice-president of marketing on the fourth floor has just discovered that someone has broken into her file cabinet. A laptop computer and a box full of disks are missing. One of the disks contains an extremely important proposal she had been editing the day before.

It's now 9:45 A.M. The thief returns to the building. He waves to the security guard in the lobby, joins an elevator discussion about the robbery, gets off at the fourth floor, and goes directly to the vice-president's office to commiserate with his colleague.

Regrettably, this scenario is not farfetched. Any manager considering potential spies should begin the search at the next desk. An insider has much better knowledge of, and access to, sensitive company information than an outsider. Moreover, insiders are protected by their co-workers' natural reluctance to think that a spy may be in their midst.

Anyone can be involved in business espionage—if not as a sole perpetrator or a key member of a spy ring, then as an intimidated collaborator or innocent dupe. Since insiders can be so easily tempted and exploited, and can do such potentially extensive damage, they deserve closer scrutiny.

THREATS FROM INSIDE THE COMPANY

Personality conflicts within an organization can often trigger business espionage. A West Coast private detective agency was visited by a health care professional from a government organization. He explained to the owner of the agency that a "war of egos" was raging at his company. The health care worker had filed a report against another employee for not doing her job. She had countered by filing a report against him, supported by a colleague who was also her good friend. All parties concerned had been gathering ammunition in anticipation of the administrative hearings and other actions that go with firing a public employee.

At this point, the health care professional was so much at odds with the two other employees that he thought they might have bugged his car. A thorough examination of the car revealed no bug. Later, however, a detective from the agency discovered that the health care worker's phone was tapped and that his rivals in the office war were having him followed.

Employees trying to further their own careers at the expense of others may also resort to espionage. This problem often surfaces when companies reorganize and large numbers of promotions, reassignments, and terminations are at stake. A middle manager suffers particular stress under these conditions since the next step may be a big one, and several highly qualified people are likely to be vying for the same position.

A former bank branch manager told a story that illustrates this point. During an interview for a position as a financial director with a government agency, he confided that he had been "aced out" of the bank by another manager during a major reorganization. He did not find out about it until later, and then only by chance. The victorious manager always stood out at meetings, especially brainstorming sessions and other supposedly off-the-cuff discussions. Time after time, he had all the relevant facts and figures at his fingertips and seemed to know what all the other managers were doing or thinking.

After the former branch manager lost the competition, he discovered that the winning manager had clandestinely paid a computer expert to modify one of the bank's software programs so that it flagged hot items through a coding system known only by him. The customized software program keyed on words like "reorganization" and "change" as it read bank correspondence and in-house communications.

There is nothing wrong, of course, with an honest manager taking full advantage of the technological capabilities at hand to make an organization more profitable. Shortchanging the organization by not sharing potentially useful information, or by using organizational technology secretly to further one's own career, is another matter.

Interpersonal espionage is damaging enough to the overall morale and productivity of a company. Even more troublesome is espionage aimed at putting the company itself in jeopardy. Individual employees may turn to espionage against their employer as a means of satisfying their curiosity, acting out a sense of superiority, supplementing their income, championing a cause, retaliating for perceived mistreatment, or "buying" a more desirable job with a rival firm. Often, however, an employee is abetting spy work that jeopardizes the company without even being aware of it.

Employees who talk too much pose a major, ongoing threat to a company's security. Salespeople are notoriously guilty of revealing company secrets inadvertently as they enrich their spiel to impress or entertain a prospective customer. An equally serious, though unrecognized, danger lies in the unguarded remarks that any employee may make outside of a strict working context. It is amazing how much confidential information is given away in ordinary social conversations. One innocent ride down the public elevator of an office building revealed these company tidbits:

1. *Mr. X, a married man, has hired his former girlfriend as his personal secretary and they have been seen at local bars together after working hours.* If this gossip fell into the wrong ears, it could tip off surveillance of Mr. X by a rival firm intent on blackmail.

2. *The Z Messenger Service is very reliable; deliveries are made every day at exactly 10:00 A.M.* Harmless as this observation may sound, a business spy would be thrilled to know exactly when the messenger arrives at a target company. The spy may wear business clothes, carry company materials in the crook of an arm, wait by the elevator at 10:00 A.M., and stop the incoming messenger with a "Hey, I'll sign for that!" The spy can then photograph the papers in a rest room before having a second messenger, or someone who looks like a messenger, deliver them to their real destination.

Idle chatter within work areas can keep a snoop regularly informed of the habits, plans, and whereabouts of key managers and executives. A conventional hearing aid can increase the listening range of an eager eavesdropper to include the voices of people who would assume they were safely distant. News acquired in this manner—even comments that seem completely innocuous to the speaker—can offer important leads to someone engaged in business espionage.

A spy who learns that Associate Director Y has just gone out of town can approach her secretary, financial aide, or management trainee and say, "Ms. Y and I were discussing the Z situation. She was going to leave the information for me before she went away. It's probably on her desk. Would you get it for me, please?" Chances are that the person will think the boss forgot to supply the information in the rush of leaving and will dig it out for the spy. It's an old, old strategem, but it works time after time.

THREATS FROM OUTSIDE: THE UNDERCOVER SPY

As you can see from these examples, it's difficult to make a clear distinction between internal and external security threats. A threat may originate inside the workplace—thanks to an employee who is vulnerable, unscrupulous, or careless—but wind up serving an outside interest. Much more common is the internal threat that is created and nourished by external forces.

Moles—crooked undercover spies-for-hire—are a fascinating breed. However varied their individual motivations may be, their methods of operation are strikingly similar. Usually, they assume a relatively insignificant job or role in a target company and affect a personality that doesn't inspire suspicion. Then they gather as much inside information as they can and sell it to a competitor. Sometimes they act on their own initiative, hoping to market what they discover to the highest bidder. At other times they are paid from the start to infiltrate a company by a rival firm with a predetermined objective.

The case histories of two composite characters—Just Plain Bill, a business spy on a week-long undercover operation as a janitor, and Our Gal Sal, a business spy on a longer assignment as an administrative assistant—reflect the most prevalent techniques moles use to ply their trade.

Case History 3: Just Plain Bill

Business managers and executives are too busy to give more than a passing glance to janitors. Those involved with espionage know this and often trade their conservative office clothes and business school manners for gray coveralls and a more folksy approach that makes them almost invisible to people working in a corporate environment.

Just Plain Bill really is a janitor in the sense that he is on the list for fill-in work with a janitorial service. This connection gives him good cover training as well as possible leads. This week, however, he is impersonating a janitor in a financial services company at the request of a rival financier. Before he leaves home, he checks his equipment:

- *Coveralls. The coveralls Bill wears over his pants are two sizes too large so that he can store spy equipment in his pants pockets and under his belt. The name of the janitorial service used by the target company is sewn on the back of the coveralls. Bill buys name patches from the same suppliers his victims do. He can also find discarded coveralls or uniforms with company logos in local thrift stores.*

- *Keys. Bill used to make duplicate keys in his truck during breaks, but then he learned a much simpler technique via spy shoptalk: He now places a piece of colored plastic tape over the DO NOT DUPLICATE sign on keys and lets a hardware store make his copies for him. The plastic tape is interpreted as a color code and is seldom questioned, even by the most scrupulous key makers.*

- *Personal cartridge-style copier. Bill has a power adapter for the copier in the back of his truck. If companies don't lock their copy machines after hours or log their number of copies, Bill uses their equipment.*

- *Bugging equipment. An FM wireless microphone, a small FM receiver, and a voice-activated recorder are standard equipment for Bill. He owns much more complicated gear; but he knows that in most instances simpler is better—easier to buy, easier to service, and harder to trace back to him.*

Finished with his prework check, Bill puts his bugging equipment into small, heavy-duty plastic bags and seals them with the electric Seal-A-Meal unit found in many kitchens. Then he hops into his truck and is off to his assignment.

Bill pulls up to the loading dock to find a security guard on duty. He dumps his plastic bags of bugging equipment into a partly filled 5-gallon bucket marked STRIPPER and walks by the guard with a grin. He knows the guard will not come too close to a bucket of strong chemicals, if only because he must pay to buy and clean his own uniform.

Bill begins work by planting the bug, since the sooner it is out of his hands, the less likely that something will go wrong to expose him. In the janitor's closet, he rinses the plastic bags protecting his equipment, tears them open, and puts the bug in his inside pocket. Now that he's past the security guard, he can risk having bulges in his coveralls. He unlocks the boardroom, lays a dust cloth on the boardroom table, and plants the bug in the ceiling. It takes exactly forty-six seconds. The bug will pick up everything said in the boardroom and transmit it to the voice-activated recorder in the janitor's closet down the hall. Bill can come back at any time to pick up full tapes and replace them with empty ones.

Next, Bill goes through all the wastebaskets next to shredders, since these are likely to contain the most important information. Many shredders simply layer the documents into a wastebasket without stirring them up. Bill carefully lifts each layer of shredded paper off the stack and places it in a clear plastic binder insert for later examination. When he's finished with the wastebaskets, he tucks the filled inserts back under his coveralls.

In one department, Bill discovers a new pulverizer that grinds confidential papers rather than just shredding them. On the assumption that this must be a hot area, he scrutinizes desk calendars, notepads, message spindles, and papers that are stuck beneath desk blotters, taking special note of informal, handwritten marks like stars, checks, and underlinings. Knowing that passwords, codes, and combinations are most often hidden within 15 feet of the equipment they access, Bill closely examines these areas as well.

Bill follows five guidelines in searching offices:

1. He will search executive offices if he has time, but only after he has searched the desks of executive secretaries. A company president may or may not have the keys to the office or the codes to operate electronically controlled office systems, but his or her secretary certainly will. Like sergeant majors in the army, secretaries may not make the big decisions, but they do run the place.

2. At some point during his search of each work area, Bill always sits at the person's desk. Computer codes are often within arm's reach of the terminal. Keys or combinations to filing cabinets or safes are usually kept where they can be reached without getting up. So are important papers that come in late and are stashed out of sight so the worker won't have to reopen the safe.

3. When finished with searching a given work area, Bill always strikes imaginary lines to other important parts of the office. Keys and access codes are often hidden somewhere in a straight line between one workstation and another.

4. Bill keeps his eyes out for accounting and bookkeeping records. They often reveal more about a company than office memos or almost anything else—and in more concise form.

5. When searching an office, Bill never gives up if he doesn't get immediate results. There is no such thing as a secret hiding place. He systematically starts in one corner of an office and

moves every item, one at a time. He examines each item carefully and puts it back exactly as he found it.

It's time for Bill to leave. Employees who work after hours must file past the security guard, but this is no problem for Bill. He sticks a big wad of chewing tobacco in his mouth. When he gets to the guard, he offers him some as he swings his head from side to side and leans toward the wastepaper basket next to the guard's desk. The guard looks disgusted, says "Outside!" and holds the door open for him. Bill grins, spits in the gutter, and heads for his truck. He'll be back.

Case History 4: Our Gal Sal

Our Gal Sal is a mole who specializes in infiltrating companies as an administrative assistant. In many companies this job title has replaced the title of secretary. The position has come to include more technological know-how and office management expertise, and represents a workforce (still predominantly female) that seeks more meaningful responsibilities. Since administrative assistants come and go in an organization with relative frequency, the job is a perfect cover for a spy on a mission of several weeks to several months.

Managers love administrative assistants, because they are skilled and flexible enough to be moved around as needed. These qualities are especially valuable to a company undergoing rapid change—precisely the kind of environment that fosters high-level espionage. Many male managers love Our Gal Sal in particular, because she offers top-notch work performance as well as submissive, flirtatious, ego-feeding camaraderie. In short, Our Gal Sal plays a role comfortably akin to the stereotype of the preliberation secretary—and she is amply rewarded for her performance. No one suspects that Our Gal Sal is devious, or even smart. She simply has a cold-blooded intelligence and a long history of sexual prejudice in her favor.

Our Gal Sal works on one job until she has uncovered all that a client wants, or all that she feels she needs to interest a potential client. At that time, she quits. She carefully cultivates a somewhat flaky image so that people aren't surprised to hear that she's leaving. After all, they've seen her circulate freely around the workplace, chatting with everyone and sighing over her dreamy visions of the future. This kind of easygoing, confidence-sharing behavior suckers in many a vulnerable colleague.

Sal does her fair share of snooping for important scraps of spoken and written information, but her primary interest is in finding weak links in the chain of workers. People are far more valuable to spies than facts and figures, and Sal's personal chain gang includes some highly representative types.

■ Sal understands the critical value of training and always lets clients know how she is broken into a new job, and by whom. Trainers often have a broader view of a company than do individual managers within the firm, though they are usually not recognized or rewarded for this special attribute. Ms. H, a disgruntled trainer, may be overlooked by management, but not by a management spy like Sal.

■ Sal observes that District Manager B habitually shirks his decision-making duties by putting things off or leaving them to subordinates. She knows that one person's indecisiveness creates a hole in the power structure that can be exploited. "Power lies in the streets!" was the rallying cry during the Russian Revolution. Sal knows that in many business companies, power lies in the aisles!

■ Sal determines that Office Manager R, who is trying to get a better job, is using the new computer scanner and laser printer to alter diplomas and other credentials that she has pilfered from the personnel file. Sal confronts Office Manager R, who suddenly can't say no when Sal wants to borrow her keys. Sal soon has the run of the place.

■ Sal discovers that Vice-President T has a secret—a second business of the same type, developed from target company contacts that he keeps for himself. Sal "innocently" leads him to admit it, and acts suitably impressed when he does. Dishonest undercover agents are constantly on the alert for recruits. An exposed thief in a company has no real choice but to cooperate, and the crooked client then gets two spies for one on the deal.

Our Gal Sal is not above using her sex appeal in her spy work, and the prelib stereotype of the loose-and-easy secretary plays right into her hands. Regrettably, many men continue to cherish this image to their own misfortune, as these examples show.

■ *Sal goes out of her way to tease and flatter Manager M— someone she has identified as being insecure and ambitious. When Manager M suggests taking Sal away for a ski weekend, she is quick to respond: "How in the world can you afford to pay for both of us when you have two kids in college?" Manager M begins bragging about how well he and the company are doing, and the subject becomes a running theme in future discussions. Manager M eventually feels so at ease with Sal that he makes business calls from her apartment.*

■ *Sal talks openly of her double dates in the presence of Director D, who controls vital company information and is married. Eventually, Director D asks Sal to set up a date for him, and she agrees. She can then use evidence of this date as blackmail. Sometimes Sal arranges a date for an unwitting male executive. He thinks he is meeting a woman by chance, but Sal has bought and paid for her in advance. A chance romantic encounter with a "presentable someone" of the opposite sex may be forgiven by a spouse or an employer, but the odds go against forgiveness if the presentable someone turns out to be a prostitute. Of course, Sal can employ the same basic strategy on any person—male or female, straight or gay. No one will believe that the victims didn't know they were consorting with prostitutes.*

The stories of Just Plain Bill and Our Gal Sal are based on what countermeasures experts have observed to be the most common manifestations of the most prevalent type of spy-for-hire. Some of these people make careers of spying and some go on to other things. Those who work undercover for long periods of time and on many different assignments, like their legitimate counterparts, learn a number of interesting facts about human nature. Managers concerned with unmasking spies are wise to pay attention to some of the things these undercover agents have learned.

■ *Simple stories close to the truth work best.* If an agent can be readily identified as a perennial student rotating shifts to fit his classes or a frustrated artist who can't make a living and so is working in the mail room, people will fit the agent into that niche and go on about their business. The "perennial student" then does not appear out of place in a menial position that allows him to float around the company at different hours, and the "frustrated artist" can then make sketches or notes for her undercover report and not attract attention.

■ *People tend to talk freely in front of those they think are not as smart as they are.* This holds true for face-to-face conversations as well as conversations in which the supposedly less intelligent person is simply within listening range. People are especially careless when talking on the phone, thinking that those around them cannot understand what is being said because only one end of the dialogue can be heard.

■ *People are not likely to notice what is above or below eye level.* A file clerk sorting folders on the floor, a janitor changing bulbs in an overhead fixture, an assembly line worker taking a break-time nap a few steps higher up the stairwell than his co-workers, or a warehouse stacker reading a book on top of a pile of boxes can see and hear some astonishing things.

■ *A story planted in advance will not be questioned; the same story told on the spur of the moment will be.* An employee-spy who suddenly quits or just drops out of sight after an undercover operation looks very suspicious. The spy who confides to co-workers, "I think I may have a better job lined up," can leave in a few days without raising an eyebrow.

THREATS FROM OUTSIDE: SNOOPS, CON ARTISTS, AND TRASH COLLECTORS

The simplest form of externally generated espionage is the covert outside surveillance of a company by a competitor. Using its own personnel or hired help, the competitor may only be fishing for information that isn't available in the public domain. It's amazing how much a spy on this type of mission can discover simply by standing on the sidelines and watching, with or without the aid of equipment. The nice old gentleman standing outside the fence while the data center is being built will know a great deal about it—even down to the wiring if critical areas are not screened.

If a company can be at risk before it even opens its doors, think of what can happen when it invites the risk factor for an inside visit. A group of undercover agents accompanying a tour of a major manufacturing facility noticed one member of the tour charting building and room layouts on graph paper. Their suspicions rose when they saw that he was using blueprint symbols and special terminology that a member of this particular tour group could not be expected to know. Tours at this facility are now severely limited!

Salespeople for Avalon Industries Inc., a Brooklyn-based toy manufacturer, were once strongly encouraged to make tours of competing plants under assumed identities. Several of these salespeople, posing as potential customers who had invented a game that required crayons, got inside rival companies and obtained valuable data about their manufacturing processes. To increase the effectiveness of their "tour spies," Avalon designed and conducted special workshops to familiarize them with different types of machinery used in the industry. A suspicious competitor finally got wise and blew the whistle.

Other visitors besides those in tour groups may also be spies, as a recent, highly publicized case of international business espionage makes clear. On a supposedly social visit to a friend who worked at an Italian subsidiary of Dow Chemical, a spy managed to steal the secret formula for a new antibiotic, which he then sold through a Swiss intermediary to the Chong Kun Dang Corporation, a giant South Korean pharmaceuticals firm. The spy's strategy was masterfully sneaky: While chatting with his friend, he "accidentally" dropped his handkerchief into a vat full of the fermenting antibiotic. He quickly recovered his handkerchief and minutes later walked out of the factory with a sample of Dow's yet-to-be-released wonder drug for combating tuberculosis.

Another major threat from outside is the bogus survey, advertisement, or proposal used to lure unsuspecting personnel into revealing the inner workings of their organizations. Unfortunately, it is almost impossible to distinguish the honest pollsters, solicitors, and negotiators, who perform a valuable service in the business community, from their crooked impersonators, who take advantage of people's trust and openness in order to betray them.

One of the most popular and effective interviewing methods in the business world today—and one most often subverted to serve the ends of business espionage—is the Delphi technique. The method, named after the ancient oracle of Apollo at Delphi, Greece, was developed by Olaf Helmer and Norman Dalkey, mathematicians at the Rand Corporation. In simple terms, the Delphi interview involves four steps:

1. Poll experts on a subject separately and in private regarding both their rational projections and their gut-reaction hunches.
2. Repeat the interview questions several times if possible, after the experts have had a chance to think about and reevaluate their data.
3. Break the data down to isolate a group opinion on the target area of interest. (Those being questioned may or may not know the questioner's true agenda.)
4. Bring together those polled to reach a consensus.

There are many possible variations of the Delphi technique, some of which the original designers would no doubt find appalling. Early in my career, when I was a management intern in one of the world's largest private detective agencies, I was the intended victim of a phony interviewer who used a modified version of this technique.

A very personable young man in conservative business clothes came to the detective agency purportedly to ask about a possible need for armored car or courier services. (The "vendor approach" is a common modus operandi for a business spy.) He gave what sounded like a memorized presentation and then began with the checklist prepared by his employer. The first few questions were very general and apparently designed to blunt the edge of skepticism. By the time he was halfway down the first page, the line of questioning had changed.

Typically, each question was a double-edged sword. The first part went something like "Is there ever a time when your company might need a courier or armored car service?" The second part then zeroed in on more sensitive information: "If so, under what circumstances?" The researcher was also interested in gut reactions. It is easy to be lulled into talking too much or to be sidetracked into giving out confidential information when an interviewer seems to be concerned with personal feelings, not just official statements.

The questions that this particular phony vendor asked are a good indication of what a spy tries to learn during an interview. For example:

Q: How often might you need courier service and for what purpose: cash, checks, or documents? How may we serve you?

The fact is that agency personnel took turns going to the bank for cash every two weeks. The bookkeeper broke the payroll down into so many $100 bills, so many $50 bills, and so on, with separate lists to coordinate individual payments. This made it very difficult for outsiders to determine the size of the agency, the way it did business, or how often staff members traveled. Had the interviewer led me into a discussion of how the agency handled cash, checks, and other documents, I might have committed a serious breach of security.

Q: Which departments of your company are most likely to need courier service? Please list them all.

The answer to this question would reveal a great deal about the internal workings of the firm, its size, and how it is structured.

Q: Which departments of your company are least likely to use courier or armored car services? What new services might we offer that would be useful to these departments?

This two-part question is brother to the question before it. Asking for crucial information one step at a time is a common practice in spy research. It is less blatant than direct questioning and also serves as a cross-check of previous information.

As a management intern, I of course saw many things within the agency that I thought needed improving and had schemes aplenty to bring about these improvements. If I had yielded to the promptings of the researcher's questionnaire, combined with his use of the Delphi technique to disorient me, I might have exposed some of the agency's most vital business secrets. This kind of thing can happen to anyone in a business context, but it's particularly likely to happen to trainees (who are told to handle the matter because they have time on their hands), to purchasing agents (whose jobs involve checking out what products and services are available), and to people in public relations (who exercise more than usual patience with outside intrusions).

The blind newspaper ad is another highly successful ploy used by outside con artists. Typically the ad offers an exciting employment opportunity in the same field as that of the client company. Résumés and application forms from employees of rival firms pour in. If they do nothing else, they reveal which employees are dissatisfied with their present jobs, what their areas of responsibility are, and how to appeal to their professional objectives. Some applicants may be invited to go through mock interviews that entice them to reveal proprietary information about their companies. They may even wind up being hired by a competitor to provide inside information about their former employer.

A more elaborate, upscale trap used in business espionage is the phony business proposal. A spy posing as an independent "whiz kid" broker or a representative of a legitimate organization contacts a target company's executives and offers them tantalizing deals—franchises, mergers, and financial maneuvers of all kinds—to lure the executives into providing data about their company. In the spy trade this scam is called "the three seeks":

1. Seek talks with every key person at the target company to get as much initial information as possible.
2. Seek printed information from the target company (such as graphs, drawings, prospectuses, and financial statements) to clarify what has been learned.
3. Seek impossible concessions near the end of the negotiations, but only after the target company has provided all the data it is likely to share.

One victim of the three seeks—a junior vice-president in a big-name firm—did an elaborate presentation for a "broker" whose only business assets were a handsome smile and a stylishly furnished, rented office. The broker was given an inch-thick folder of documents that began with a history of the company and ended with future plans. The facts and figures were beautifully presented: a work of art that went to an artful thief.

At the opposite end of the spectrum from the phony broker is the trash connoisseur. Next to the telephone, the wastebasket represents the most important information pipeline a clever business spy can use. Chapter 2 detailed the case of amateur garbologist Marc Feith, Hillenbrand Industries' spy-turned-counterspy, whose methodology was fairly uninspired. Here are two variations of the treasure-in-the-trash hunt that are a bit more imaginative. After all, the security risks surrounding discarded papers and materials are high for virtually any kind of business organization.

Case History 5: Willie the Wino

The target company was a fast-growing newcomer in the communications industry—a highly competitive field that generates a great deal of paper, despite the fact (or perhaps because of the fact) that this is the Computer Age. A competitor wanted very much to get a look at some of this paper, but wanted to do it from outside the company and with a minimum of trouble.

The two spies hired by the competitor quickly focused their attention on a large dumpster just off the end of the target company's main loading dock. On raid night Willie, the dumpster spy, put on his wino outfit. His partner, who was dressed in a suit, drove him out to the target company and parked up the street. Willie the Wino wandered over and sat on the edge of the dumpster. When he was sure that no one was watching, he tumbled in and set up shop. Two old paper bags, a penlight, extra batteries, and lunch were all the equipment he needed—plus his knowledge of normal office procedures.

Willie checked colored paper first. If office memos in the executive wing are blue, that narrows things down. If the accounting department uses yellow, that helps too. So Willie began to sort by color while he dug carefully through all the layers of paper. He was searching for batches of paper from specific, predetermined areas within the company and didn't want to mix them with other, less interesting materials. The contents of wastebaskets and other trash containers tend to remain together when upended into a dumpster, even one the size of a room.

The trick for Willie was to be systematic. He found a letter written on the high-quality, watermarked, 20-pound bond that companies usually reserve for important documents. He lifted a fistful from that section of the dumpster and riffled the edges, much as a gambler might do with a deck of cards. By slanting the "deck" and sighting along the edges, Willie was able to distinguish the high-quality bond stationery and sort it out. Separate stacks of colored paper and executive stationery rose around him.

A janitor came out on the loading dock with a wheelbarrow full of paper from one of the upper floors. He spoke to the night guard, who remained at his desk just inside the door when he wasn't making predictable, punch-clock rounds. Willie slid a piece of cardboard over his piles of sorted paper and dug down out of sight. The janitor rolled the wheelbarrow up the ramp, tipped it into the dumpster, and left.

So far so good. Willie had a drink of water from a clean wine bottle and ate part of a sandwich he had brought in one of his shopping bags. He had been in the dumpster three hours. As he ate, he glanced at some personal handwritten notes on the off chance that they would give him a clue as to who was doing what with whom. Something seemed to be going on between a man whose first initial was G and a woman named Barbara.

Willie had been in the dumpster more than four hours when he heard the two short warning blasts from the distinctive horn of his partner's car. ("Double for trouble" has been a warning code since frontier days.) Someone in the target company had seen his penlight from an upper window; or maybe the guard, stepping out for a smoke, had spotted him.

Willie stuffed the 30 pounds of paper he had sorted from the trash into his shopping bags. He sat in the corner of the dumpster clutching his wine bottle as the security guard and a night foreman from the target company approached. Willie barely had time to mumble something to them before his partner drove up, flashed a security badge he had bought from a mail-order house, and grabbed him by the collar.

"We've been looking for this son of a bitch for questioning," his partner explained to the two company men. "Thanks for your help. I'll take it from here." To Willie, he shouted, "Get in the back seat, you bastard!" Willie and his partner disappeared with two shopping bags of goodies before the company men had time to think twice about it.

The two spies drove out to a rented garage and spent the rest of the night sorting the stolen documents into small batches. Those from each target area designated by the client went into separate folders. The papers in each file were then broken down by individual employees. A senior planner identified by other documents as "George" was clearly the man who had received the compromising, handwritten note from "Barbara." The note itself had been torn in two before being thrown away. Willie always gave extra scrutiny to torn or defaced documents: People instinctively treat sensitive papers to special abuse when they're discarding them.

Willie and his partner placed mail sent to the target company by other firms in a separate folder for cross-reference. Managers who maintain good controls within their own organizations would be horrified to learn how lightly their secrets are regarded by their business associates. An order form or letter that lays bare the inner workings of a company is often just one more piece of trash to its recipient. Even law firms sometimes casually discard their clients' privileged information. Maybe it is just human nature for people to consider other people's secrets less important than their own.

Information that is easy to obtain can be just as marketable as information that is very troublesome to obtain: As in any marketing effort, presentation counts for a lot. Willie uses a household iron to smooth out the more sensational documents and binds them in a special folder. With this marketing ploy, their past history as garbage is obliterated, the client is impressed, and Willie continues to reap great profit from his work.

Case History 6: Diplo the Dino

Preliminary spy work aimed at a highly diversified manufacturing company revealed that most of its high-quality used paper was baled in a special machine and trucked directly to a paper dealer for recycling. As all good spies know, a secret loses its confidential status in direct proportion to the distance it travels from the personal control of whoever first deemed it a secret. The two spies involved in this case correctly surmised that what was confidential correspondence within the walls of the target company would be inconsequential scrap paper by the time it reached the recycling warehouse across town.

The spies drove to the warehouse in a rented truck and entered the main office carrying a foot-high, papier-mâché dinosaur. The dialogue between the spy and the warehouse manager went like this:

S: Our students' school project for the year is dinosaurs. We want to buy some bales of scrap paper for papier-mâché.

M: Dinosaurs?

S: Yes. Like this one, only much bigger. Isn't he cute? You tear paper into little pieces, soak it in water, and layer it over a frame of chicken wire. The children in my classes always enjoy making things from papier-mâché.

M: Dinosaurs?

S: Yes. We need enough paper to make a big Diplodocus, like this one, and a Tyrannosaurus, at least. There are about fifty children in the two classes, and we need white paper so we can paint the finished dinosaurs with watercolors.

M: Diplodocus?

S: Yes. Do you have bales of used white paper we can buy and take with us now? We rented a truck.

M: I don't know nothing about dinosaurs. We usually only sell by the ton; but since it's for the kids, I guess it's okay. I haven't got time to sort it out, but the white high-rag stuff is over against that wall. Pick out a bale or two if you like and I'll have someone load it with a forklift for you. Just don't break no bales. They're packed under pressure and the strapping could whip around and slice your head off. You can tell what's inside by looking at the paper on the ends. Give me a yell when you're ready to load.

The spies left Diplo the Dino on the office counter to validate their pretext and spent more than an hour in the salvage warehouse looking for bales from the target company. No one hurried them. When they found what they were looking for, they had it loaded in their truck, paid a nominal fee, and left. It took many hours to sort through this 400-pound windfall. When they were finished, they not only uncovered specific bits and pieces of data that made a significant whole but also gained a comprehensive view of the target company's internal structure.

First, the spies sorted by department. Everything directed to or from the executive wing went in one pile. Product research, sales, and finance each had a section. The contents of the waste-paper baskets from the security department were given special consideration.

The second step was to break down the department files by subject matter, using the guidelines already unwittingly provided by the target company. A firm's internal terminology and titles are often major clues to its management style, its business procedures, and its pet projects.

The third step was to sort the documents in each pile by the names of the target company employees who signed them. The resulting piles were left as they were, with a "to" and "from" checklist added to the top of each one to help in charting the course of a particular piece of correspondence. Had the spies chosen to work with a computer scanner, they might also have read apparently important documents into computer memory for sorting or tracking.

The piles were carefully stacked in labeled cardboard boxes. Then the spies shifted the boxes around on the concrete floor of the rented garage until a pattern began to emerge: Ms. W from the research and development department worked with Mr. N from the production department to accomplish project D5; Mr. O was in charge of final design for product C and had the keys for area 17; and so on.

One of the spies took a carefully prepared arrangement of documents to the client. His presentation rivaled that of a French chef offering a tempting new appetizer: The display and taste were stimulating, but the product was carefully designed to satisfy the customer completely. When the spy explained some of the ways the stolen information could be used, the client assumed a full-scale undercover operation was in progress and paid accordingly.

The obvious lesson to be learned from these two case histories is that a company should take extra precautions to make sure that its hard-copy waste doesn't end up revealing company secrets to an unscrupulous outsider. A less obvious lesson, perhaps, is that a great deal of business espionage requires nothing more than human ingenuity and low-tech materials. Far more important are the high-tech materials that are commonly associated with spy work: the sophisticated equipment that can see and/or hear virtually anything that goes on in a company, regardless of whether a human spy is present. These materials are the focus of Chapter 4.

The Spy Store:

Bugs, Gadgets, and Other Devices Spies Use

> "Next to knowing all about your own business, the best thing is to know all about the other fellow's business."
> **John D. Rockefeller**

During April and May of 1987, the United States and the Soviet Union became embroiled in what the press labeled the Battle of the Bugs. Washington, reeling from the scandal of alleged spying by marine guards stationed in Moscow, accused Soviet contractors of planting espionage devices in construction materials for the new U.S. chancery. "The whole building is one big microphone," claimed Hal Lipset, an expert private eye from San Francisco who won fame in the 1960s by hiding a bug in a martini olive. The snoops caught red-handed were quick to retaliate. Soviet diplomats in Washington invited the press to an exhibit of eavesdropping equipment they had uncovered inside their new embassy compound on Wisconsin Avenue.

And so it went. The U.S. Senate passed a resolution condemning the Soviet espionage strategy. Secretary of State George Schultz and Soviet Foreign Minister Eduard Shevardnadze held arms control talks in Moscow in a special trailer flown over from the United States. Meanwhile, bug-probing U.S. Representatives Dan Mica and Olympia Snowe, who accompanied Schultz, used kiddie Magic Slates to communicate inside the chancery building itself.

As a result of the short-lived embassy wars, American newspaper readers and television viewers got a crash course in state-of-the-art espionage technology. They learned how miniscule cameras secretly photograph documents that have been fed into copiers, how listening bugs hidden in chairs turn themselves on when someone sits down, and how tiny electronic transmitters can be mixed into concrete.

The American public also found out that computer technology has greatly increased both the risk of information leakage and the eavesdropping capabilities of the interested spy. On the one hand, computers give off radio waves that can be picked up by interception equipment outside a building and transferred almost simultaneously to another computer. On the other hand, computers make it possible to sort out a specific voice transmission from a supposedly noise-camouflaged soundtrack. Gone are the days of turning up the radio and whispering secrets to heavy metal songs.

The most fascinating revelation to emerge from the Battle of the Bugs was that espionage technology no longer needs to depend on specially installed listening or viewing devices. A carefully focused outside laser beam or microwave field can pick up minute signals from anything that vibrates, such as a typewriter key or a window in a room where people are talking. The signals can then be processed through a computer and "decoded."

American experts theorized that the Soviets had aimed low-level microwaves at the U.S. embassy in Moscow to pick up telltale reverberations within cavities that were built into the walls for this purpose. When he heard about these speculations, Vyacheslav Borovikov, a security officer at the Soviet embassy in Washington, countered with a story about a Soviet diplomat who innocently looked out his apartment window: "Boom! He received a laser stroke in the eye."

What all these charges and countercharges make clear is that today the walls really do have ears! What the general public may overlook, however, is that spies find the walls of private houses, offices, and factories just as vulnerable and attractive as the walls of national embassies. The more rarefied espionage tools like laser beams may not yet be in common use. But business spies love fancy gadgets, and their personal stock includes many ingenious devices about which most potential victims are dangerously ignorant. Sophisticated spy gear is not just a feature of international political intrigue—nor is it difficult to acquire.

COME SPY WITH ME

It has an impressive title: the Omnibus Crime Control Act of 1968. It covers an impressively broad territory: to use, possess, sell, advertise, or transport eavesdropping equipment is a federal crime. It even establishes an impressively stiff penalty for such a crime: five years and $10,000 plus a victim's right to civil damages. In practice, however, it continues to be one of the least effective laws on the books.

The problem with the Omnibus Crime Control Act, of course, is that it tries to impose clarity on a situation that is almost impenetrably murky. Devices that can be used illegally in private espionage can be sold legally as private security mechanisms. In any sales transaction involving such equipment, it is the responsibility of the buyer, not the seller, to consult legal counsel for interpretation of the law's applicability. The business spy, who makes a career of violating laws, is not likely to seek a lawyer's advice or to be deterred by yet another piece of legislation. Further, many espionage victims never report eavesdropping crimes, particularly since the specific, human perpetrators are almost always untraceable.

The truth is that today's spies-for-hire can buy bugging gear or anything else they may need as easily as hired assassins can find firearms. A hypothetical shopping spree with a dishonest espionage agent can reveal some valuable insights into how spies operate and how to catch them at their own game. The equipment on this shopping tour is available on the open market, but not necessarily all in one place or all from one supplier. Typically, spies get most of their devices by sending a prepared mail-order form to a post office box advertised in a magazine or catalog, or by putting together separate components sold at mass-market electronics stores like Radio Shack. It takes very little talent or inside knowledge. The manufacturers of the equipment almost always provide ample assembly instructions and helpful hints on application.

The spy on this hypothetical shopping spree is lucky enough to have found a one-stop, full-service institution called The Spy Store. For this excursion, he has drawn up a shopping list divided into three categories:

1. See a secret.
2. Hear a secret.
3. Steal a secret.

As luck would have it, The Spy Store is arranged so that he can shop for each category systematically.

See a Secret

The Spy Store has "specials" scattered throughout its aisles to tempt gadget-loving customers. Near the entrance, at Aisle 1, is a pyramid display of a hot new item: cylinders stenciled with IN-VESTIGATOR'S X-RAY CHEMICAL SPRAY in bold block letters. The small-print instructions read:

> Spray the chemical on any standard envelope. It will not affect pencil or pen marks or typewriting. After spraying, the affected area will become transparent, and the contents of the envelope will be visible for 30 to 60 seconds. The spray may be used on both sides of an envelope and will dry without a trace in a short time.

Cans of this spray can be found in many company security offices, where they're used to check suspicious packages and letters for bombs. A business spy may also use the spray on unopened mail taken from a parked car. People routinely leave their car keys with lot attendants, assuming that their car and the papers in it are safe. But this is frequently not the case, as our spy-shopper well knows. He smiles and puts one of the $9 spray cans in his shopping cart. He's off to a good start.

Our spy already has a good 35mm camera that mounts on a telescope. A custom-made bracket is clamped behind the vent in his van, a standard tripod stands behind a curtain in his office, and a folding one-legged mount goes with him into the field. The 35mm still camera, once a staple tool for those involved in espionage, no longer excites him. These days, he's much more intrigued by video systems.

Aisle 2 of The Spy Store features a portable video system complete with color camera for under $1,000. Its inexpensive videocassettes, which can easily be copied, enable the operator to bypass outside film-processing labs. The system is also lightweight and easy to use. The label mentions numerous potential applications, including the taping of "factory tours" and "sporting events." We've already seen how informative factory tours can be to a spy. As for sporting events, more than one local football coach has caught "spotters" outside the fence during a practice session just before the season's big game. Sports, too, are big business and attract their share of business spies.

The camera unit in this video system has a zoom lens, works in normal light, and is linked to a unidirectional electret condenser microphone (electret refers to a type of ultraminiature mike) that adds sound to the pictures. It also has still-frame, audio-dubbing, and automatic fine-editing capabilities, so our spy can now become a tape editor without the need to cut and splice. The system is too good for him to pass up. He puts it in his shopping cart and moves on to more exotic merchandise.

He spots a television camera 2.2 inches square by 4.53 inches long. Next to it is an even smaller television camera: 2 inches high by 2 inches wide and less than 1 inch deep from the front of the lens to the back of the camera! These tiny solid-state or chip cameras are enormously popular, with spies as well as spy-catchers. There are just too many hidden-camera models on display for our spy to make a choice right now, so he writes down their descriptions to discuss later with his cohorts.

One shelf features a wireless video surveillance camera that is invisibly and intangibly concealed in the spine of a Yellow Pages phone book. Nearby is a sign indicating that the vendor will insert the camera into the phone book of the purchaser's choice. A phone book can sit anywhere without arousing suspicion. Most often, it's placed in a work area that contains lots of other potentially interesting information, and the spine of the book almost always faces the worker for convenient reference.

Also on the shelf are four hidden-camera models that can be placed into virtually any office or factory setting without arousing suspicion: a wall-clock model, an exit-sign model, a model that looks (and functions) like a metal card file, and a smoke-alarm model. The smoke-alarm model is especially attractive to our spy. Mounted in a hallway, it can detect everyone coming and going. Mounted over a desk, it can photograph all the documents on top of the desk; and with the addition of a pinhole microphone it can listen as the documents are discussed.

The shelf also features fancier hidden-camera items that can be given to intended victims as gifts. One is an AM/FM radio with high-fidelity sound for normal listening and a built-in pinhole camera for spying. When the radio is positioned for the best sound in a room, it is also aligned for the best pictures. (A radio or speaker box is almost always positioned to face the listener and "covers" most of the room.) Another item resembles an ordinary portable television set, except that it watches the viewer whether the set is turned on or not.

In a spotlit showcase hangs a remarkably ingenious espionage tool: a standard telephone wall box with a built-in camera. Set in the lounge or laboratory of a target company, this device instantly enables a spy to see who is speaking on a bugged phone—a major breakthrough for spies in large organizations. The more faces that spies can associate with voices, the more situations they can exploit. If Jane calls to have the carpool vehicle serviced, an eavesdropper who knows what Jane looks like can tail her and bug exactly the right vehicle. If Jim calls to make an appointment with a psychic, an eavesdropper who knows what Jim looks like can bump into him and win his confidence by taking note of his special interest. This roping technique almost always garners valuable inside information, and even a co-spy.

A rack of innocent-looking attaché cases deserves closer scrutiny. Our spy already has an attaché case with a built-in hidden camera and recorder, of course, but here is something special: a case with a 1.5-inch monitor that enables its owner to review videotaped materials without having to go back to the office. Beside it is another special case: a remote-control unit equipped with an 11mm pinhole lens, a minicamera, and a wireless transmitter. A battery-operated monitor can pick up video signals from the hidden camera at distances of up to 200 feet. Our spy can now remain down the street, up on the roof, across the street in another building, or in some other safely distant place. The complete unit costs less than $4,000.

On a special display stand in the center of the aisle is one of The Spy Store's best sellers: a hidden-camera item designed to blend in with the decor of every office, computer center, workstation, and factory in the world. It is portable and can be carried anywhere without arousing suspicion. The unwitting observer sees only an ordinary black, plastic, three-ring notebook binder. In its spine is a tiny, concealed video camera. Our spy uses a lot of these binders and can't resist putting a few of them into his cart right now.

Satisfied that he has taken note of the best of the hidden-camera devices, our spy moves on to some accessories for the closed-circuit video equipment he already owns. There are cases filled with pinhole lenses: lenses that see through quarter-inch and even sixteenth-inch openings, right-angle lenses, wide-angle lenses, and automatic-iris lenses. What interests our spy most, however, are the flexible fiber-optic lenses, which can be stationed some distance away from the rest of the camera unit. Such lenses are the ideal solution for those difficult installations where the camera monitoring a room has to fit into a crawlspace under the floor, on the inside of a suspended ceiling, or around a corner in a more secluded area. The tiny lenses are virtually invisible, and the connecting cable looks much like ordinary cable found in offices, factories, and houses. Our spy puts several of these lenses into his cart.

Aisle 3 contains some of the jazzier "see a secret" stuff. One video-copy processor can make hard copies of video displays in ten seconds—a major advantage in business espionage, where speed can be crucially important. A quad selector allows the pictures from any four remote hidden cameras to be shown at the same time on the same monitor—perfect for the enterprising agent who wants to spy on several areas at the same time. Last but not least, there is yet another Spy Store special: a cordless video-audio transmitter for under $400. At less than 2 inches high, 6 inches wide, and 9 inches deep, the device is easy to conceal. For live video pictures, a spy simply connects a hidden camera to the transmitter. The transmitted pictures can be viewed on any television set tuned to UHF Channel 14. Of course, a target victim can also tune a TV set on Channel 14 and see what the hidden camera is seeing!

Night-vision equipment takes up Aisle 4, the "owl eyes" viewers that electro-optically amplify low levels of light to make night spying easier. Night-vision binoculars or telescopes allow a spy to see and photograph into darkened windows and shadowed rooms without having to use attention-getting spotlights. Accessories include a 35mm SLR camera relay lens, a video closed-circuit television adapter, and telephoto and zoom lenses. There are also weapon adapters to mount night-vision scopes on the M-16 and Heckler & Koch assault rifles, among others. Our spy takes note of some prices for later reference and moves on to the next category on his list.

Hear a Secret

Turning to Aisle 5, our spy runs into another Spy Store special—a wireless microphone for $69. It's one dime high and three dimes long and transmits on the FM band to any FM radio set at the corresponding frequency (usually somewhere between the frequencies of licensed broadcasting stations).

Thousands of these microphones are sold each year as "baby-sitters": Placed near a crib, they allow anyone in the neighborhood to check in on baby over FM radio. Thousands more wireless mikes are sold for professional entertainment purposes. No one knows how many are sold as "basic bugs." But considering how often they are found during counterespionage investigations, they're apparently far more popular with spies than with worried parents or lounge singers.

Since our spy already has plenty of basic bugs, he moves on down the aisle and examines other listening equipment. Seven clever devices catch his eye:

- A bug with an attached spike mike that can be pushed through a wall, ceiling, or floor from the other side ($88).
- A bug that will pick up sound in an adjacent room simply by touching a wall, ceiling, or floor ($80).
- A "concrete microphone" capable of clear audio reception through a 10-inch-thick cement block ($97).
- A ballpoint pen bug (which can also write) with a range of 300 to 400 yards that operates for forty hours on one set of batteries ($115).
- An FM telephone transmitter the size of an alligator clip that can be attached to telephone lines and terminals to pick up both sides of a telephone conversation ($21).

- An FM transmitter that is slightly smaller than the end joint of the little finger: not the smallest bug in the world, but the biggest bargain ($74).
- A bug that can be attached to any speaker, intercom, or telephone to transform it into a listening device, even when it is turned off ($44).

Our spy takes one of each and heads to Aisle 6, which stocks audio telescopes. These telescopes are, in effect, binoculars for the ears that build up weak or distant sounds so that they can be heard and recorded. The unit that first catches our spy's eye looks like a miniature space cannon from a sci-fi movie. In fact, it is a superdirectional microphone, small enough to be mounted on a video camera, that can pick one voice out of a crowd across the street ($69). The bigger and more complex models down the aisle suit more problematic spy situations.

Today, our spy is seeking listening devices for a specific upcoming assignment: He wants to bug a company boat that executives use for offshore, off-the-record weekend outings. Officially, these trips are for pleasure; unofficially, they include a great deal of business talk that is often more revealing than what can be heard in the boardroom.

Our spy is well aware that the range of a bug transmitting from open water is much greater than the range of a bug transmitting within a city, and the signal itself is much clearer. He also knows that pleasure boats are usually left unattended for long periods of time in areas that offer poor security. Marina guards are trained primarily to keep people from stealing objects *off* a boat, not to prevent people from getting *on* a boat, especially if they look like important guests or maintenance workers.

The first device our spy selects for this job is a strong audio telescope that will allow him to hear shipboard conversations from the shore while the boat remains within eyesight. Next, he chooses a special antenna that can be attached to the mast of the boat. Whether it's hidden or left in plain sight, it is unlikely to be discovered. Then he loads his cart with numerous small eavesdropping devices that can be easily concealed inside boating equipment or in the body of the boat itself. (Most boats have built-in hiding places that people seldom inspect.) A barometer, thermometer, or wind gauge with an outside probe or indicator, for example, makes an excellent "bug nest," since the probe or indicator functions automatically as an antenna. Fortunately, our spy knows several specialists in vehicle surveillance who can help him design the perfect systems and backup systems for his boat-bugging assignment.

With his immediate business needs satisfied, our spy turns to the many intriguing "hear a secret" accessories at the end of the aisle. Four in particular catch his fancy:

- A device resembling a pocket calculator that reads telephone numbers off tape recordings. When a spy eavesdrops on a telephone conversation, it helps to know the number the victim dialed ($450).
- A telephone autostart that engages and disengages a recorder automatically to save batteries and tape when nothing is happening on the line ($25).
- A sound-limiting preamplifier that facilitates recording in a large area with only one hidden microphone. It evens out both weak and strong sounds for better reception in such noisy settings as an industrial assembly shop, an executive dining room, and an outdoor company picnic ($79).
- An array of telephone voice changers that can be placed over a telephone handset to change the sound of the speaker's voice.

Up to his ears in listening gear, our spy turns to the third category on his list.

Steal a Secret

Aisle 7 begins with a singularly dull-looking Spy Store special: a flat metal bar that costs less than $10. A closer look reveals that this ordinary-looking item is a highly sophisticated, computer-designed tool for breaking into cars. It fits inside the door itself to defeat the locking mechanism by lifting the latch arm rather than the knob on the doorsill. These days, it's a standard tool for tow truck drivers. Our spy picks one up for his own tool kit.

So much for the crude, blunt instruments. The rest of Aisle 7 contains books, most of them high-quality technical publications. Ostensibly written to advise law enforcement or security personnel, they also serve to keep spies informed of the latest methods of sneaking into a locked house, office, factory, safe, drawer, or file cabinet. A few of the books are slipshod products of underground presses that cater more directly to the socially depraved (a class that includes our shopper). This highly interesting shelf mix includes:

- A guide to lock picking that describes methods of bypassing antipick devices, modifying locks, and making forced-entry tools.
- A book on how international smugglers acquire and market everything from designer jeans and watches to drugs and weapons.
- A government-issue paperback that shows how government agencies open mail, with chapters on "wet openings" and "dry openings."
- An exposé on the underground economy that explains how to keep two sets of financial records, how to invest unreported income, and how to skim money from aboveground businesses.
- A manual on detecting false IDs that shows how to make birth certificates, passports, driver's licenses, social security cards, and documents relating to citizenship, insurance claims, and securities investments.
- An extensive list of job opportunities in the black market, including detailed discussions of relevant skills for stakeouts, breaking and entering, fencing, loan-sharking, and flimflamming.
- A pamphlet of order blanks for satellite shots printed by the U.S. Geological Survey's Earth Resources Observation Systems (EROS)—a must for any spy interested in color-coded layouts of factory installations, industrial parks, or office building complexes.

Our spy is struck with the potential usefulness of four books in particular:

1. *Where's What: Sources of Information for Federal Investigators* (New York: Warner Books, 1976). Originally prepared by Harry J. Murphy of the CIA and now declassified, this classic book lists hundreds of sources of business information, including credit records, and offers such handy research tips as "ten questions to ask yourself in reading a Dun & Bradstreet report." The preface cautions:

> An investigator must ever realize his tremendous responsibility. On the one hand he is dealing with a most precious commodity—a man's career—and on the other hand he is working to the good of the United States government. He must conduct his inquiries in such a way as to never do a disservice to either.

This is a fine sentiment, but it holds no appeal to our spy. The book itself has great appeal!

2. *What's What* (David Fisher and Reginald Bragonier, editors, New York: Ballantine Books, 1982). This book is a visual glossary of all kinds of objects, from paper clips to passenger ships. Of particular interest to our spy are the sections on symbols of science, business, and commerce; parts of firearms, vaults, safes, and locks; and design elements of checks, credit cards, and money orders.

3. *Survival Evasion and Escape* (U.S. Government Printing Office, Army Field Manual FM 21-76, 1969). This book, like similar ones applicable to branches of the military, is a popular do-it-yourself guide for survivalists, soldiers of fortune, and other self-styled individualists, such as our spy. It contains innumerable tips for breaching security systems. Consider, for example, this instructive passage:

> To determine if a wire is electrified, use this quick and simple test. Carefully approach the wire, making no quick movements which might cause you to touch the wire accidentally. Hold a stem of grass or a damp stick on the wire. If the wire is charged, you will receive a mild shock, but will not be injured. [p. 241, (1-B)]

4. *Crime and Secrecy: The Use of Offshore Banks and Companies* (U.S. Government Printing Office, Report of the Senate Permanent Subcommittee on Investigations, 1985). This book lists twenty-nine tax havens alphabetically from Antigua to the Turks and Caicos Islands and outlines in some detail how to use "brass

plate" banks to hide funds from any source. Our spy, like most business spies, has a sizable chunk of unreportable income each year.

Our spy loads these handy reference works into his cart and moves toward the checkout counter. There he surveys the impulse items clustered near the register under a sign reading UNIQUE EXECUTIVE GIFTS. Two items stand out among the others:

- A gadget the size of a credit card, made of rust-resistant, razor-grade stainless steel, that can be used as a slashing weapon, a wire stripper, a screwdriver, a can opener, and a mirror. It can also open doors. It comes with a vinyl case that fits inside a wallet, and it sells for $6.
- The Lipstick Knife, a blade built into a lipstick case. It is 2.5 inches long, permanently sharp, and double-edged. Priced at $7, it is the perfect gift for his favorite female accomplice.

Well satisfied, for the moment at least, our spy waits his turn, pays cash for all the items in his shopping cart, and leaves The Spy Store with bundles under both arms.

SPECIAL BONUSES

It is easy to get dazzled by espionage gadgets and gizmos and lose sight of the fact that many business spies simply exploit technology that is already in place, often installed by the victims themselves. Phone tapping, for example, is easy thanks to the wiring used by phone companies. Most phone lines come equipped with two extra wires (called the "spare pair" in the trade) that clever tappers can use for eavesdropping.

Virtually every business phone exchange has an electronic switching (ES) system to allow for call-waiting and other special services. These systems are programmed to send out an identifying code ahead of any call so the phone company can automatically sort out a particular client company's calls from the thousands of calls on a given trunk line. With a simple bug, a business spy can do the same thing.

James A. Ross, a New York–based engineer who holds corporate seminars on business espionage, recalls the story of one client, the president of a major manufacturing firm. The executive began to suspect that he was a victim of spy activity after he lost out on $200 million worth of bids to the federal government. The client was right. When Ross and his associates "swept" the client's office, they discovered that his speaker phone had been wired to his office's spare pair.

In this case, the existing technology ended up benefiting not just the spy but the victim himself. Since the winning bidder happened to be the client's landlord, there was little doubt that he was the culprit. To make sure of this, Ross suggested leaving the bug intact and feeding it with false information that could lead the spy to reveal himself inadvertently. (Ross tells all his clients to refer to sweeps as "paint jobs" when talking in their offices so that any eavesdroppers will assume that their bugs are still safe.)

"You know what the president did?" Ross snorted. "Nothing. He'd probably been playing footsie with the competition or had a girlfriend on the side. And now he knew that the spy had all the info on him."

The telephone isn't the only technological device that can turn against an office occupant. Even the basic wiring can become a spy hotline. The biggest sensation in the business espionage world since the fiber-optic lens is the wireless transmitter/speaker system. All a spy has to do is plug a tiny transmitting device into an AC outlet in a room and all sounds from that room will travel through the building's wiring. In order to hear the sounds, the spy simply plugs a tiny speaker into any of the other outlets in the building.

In December 1985, F. T. Marotta, a colorful East Coast corporate private eye, told *Manhattan, Inc.* reporter Ron Rosenbaum about a merger case that involved this clever espionage mechanism. His story bears repeating, since it offers an entertaining view of a typical undercover investigation with some unusual twists. Here is Marotta's account:

> This case involved a *Fortune* 500 company, and it was set up in such a way that another PI came up to me and said, "I can't handle this. I want to give it to you, but it's so sensitive that what we'll do is this: The principal will meet you at Grand Central at three o'clock by the Kodak sign, and he'll be wearing a pin-striped suit and carrying a briefcase which will be

standing next to him, and a newspaper will be lying on top of it." Real James Bond stuff! "There's a reason for this," he's telling me. "You'll walk up to him, and at that moment you two will decide where you're going to go."

So I did all this. I met the guy and he said to me, "I am the president of a company, and we are going to be making a move that will put us in the top 20 of the *Fortune* 500 list based on a merger negotiation that's taking place, and I've gotten wind of information leaking out on this negotiation. The meeting on which it all hinges is scheduled to take place on such-and-such a date, and it is imperative that only the people directly involved in the negotiation know. I believe that someone has information that will damage this negotiation."

The company president explained to Marotta that he suspected the information could only be leaking from a single conference room. Here Marotta recalls his reply to the president, and what happened next.

What we have to do is come in and do a complete electronic sweep of the entire place and a physical search, and if there is a bug, we isolate it and know exactly where it's going. I told him it had to be done in the middle of the night when we have total control and there's nobody there. So we went in as telephone repairmen, four of us. Security was unbelievably lax; we didn't have to sign anything. We spent two days—a total of 35, maybe 40 hours—sweeping that place.

We found a bug in the conference room, and it was an ingenious one. You have a socket, and in the socket you have a double-gang outlet that has two openings. You can get the outlet replaced with something that looks exactly like it that transmits a room conversation anywhere along the AC line. So we took a Polaroid of it to show the client it was there, but we never disconnected it. When we showed him the Polaroid, he went white. The reality of the situation made him physically ill. I said to him, "You know two things now: Your conversations are bugged and the leak isn't coming from one of the people in the conference room; otherwise they wouldn't need the bug."

Marotta then presented his client with a plan to ensure the safety of the final deal making:

I said to him, "You want this merger to happen? This is exactly what you do. You leave the bug in place. Don't tip them off. Go through all your meetings in the same way, but hold back the key information until the last two meetings, and I'll tell you exactly how to handle them."

When it came time for those final meetings, Marotta again met with his client and explained his plan:

You get everybody in the conference room and you say, "We're going to lunch." You'll have three limos downstairs, which I'll provide from three different companies. And only then, when you're all in the limos, I'll come by and tell you exactly where to go for lunch. That way there's no way anyone can know ahead of time where it's going to be and no one can plant a bug there.

The client thought Marotta was absolutely crazy, but he went through with the plan and the merger took place.

By now it should be clear exactly who business spies are, what they want, and how they operate. The next step is to consider both some commonsensical and some not so commonsensical ways that potential victims can counteract business espionage. Chapters 5–9 examine strategies for preventing and discouraging business espionage in advance; for detecting if, when, and how business espionage is happening; and for defusing a business espionage situation so that it works to the intended victim's benefit instead of the spy's.

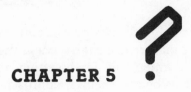

CHAPTER 5

The Countermeasures Manager:

A Starter's Kit for Spy-Proofing Your Business

> *"Originality is simply a fresh pair of eyes."*
> **Woodrow Wilson**

Corporate security is at a crisis point—possibly its biggest crisis point in the history of American business. The current wave of leveraged buyouts, mergers, acquisitions, downsizings, and technological conversions has increased espionage opportunities and rewards dramatically. But this is not the main problem. The same tumultuous climate has forced security departments, like other corporate functions, to justify their usefulness or else suffer severe cutbacks.

Unfortunately, security departments are at a distinct disadvantage here. In most business organizations security officers operate behind the scenes and are perceived as semi-independent specialists rather than as members of the mainstream management team. Not only do senior executives tend to ignore security departments unless a particularly calamitous loss or crime occurs; they also fail to devise accurate methods for identifying their security needs and determining whether existing security measures are effective. The unhappy, ironic, and almost inconceivable result is that many organizations are reducing their security staffs and eliminating security procedures at a time when security risks appear to be greater than ever.

In a business world of volatile and often conflicting changes, it is imperative for every manager to become a countermeasures manager: a businessperson committed to playing a responsible, informed role in thwarting and combating business espionage. This entrepreneurial approach is the only way managers can be sure that their companies, their projects, and their careers are safe.

Even organizations that are enlightened enough to hire official, full-time countermeasures managers have no security guarantees. All other managers must actively cooperate with these specialists in designing, implementing, and assessing security activities and goals. Otherwise, they will be passively making the system weaker for themselves, their colleagues, and their clients.

What exactly do countermeasures managers do? Simply stated, their role is to:

- Conduct security surveys and loss-prevention audits.
- Set security objectives and policies as well as ethical standards for conducting business.
- Design plans, procedures, and controls to protect assets, operations, and personnel.
- Hire and train security and investigative specialists.
- Compose security guides and manuals.
- Lead discussions about security issues and business ethics among staff members.

Ultimately, the countermeasures role can extend to every aspect of the organization as the manager works to integrate the security function with corporate planning, marketing, financing, legal administration, human resources, data processing, and so on.

THE PEOPLE PERSPECTIVE

Physical security will always be the major line of defense against business espionage, and property protection will inevitably remain the most compelling antiespionage strategy. It is only logical for a manager to be primarily concerned with controlling access to important data and equipment, keeping them under lock and key when not in use, and posting guards, surveillance devices, and/or alarm systems at all entry points to areas where such data and equipment are stored. Nonetheless, the effective countermeasures manager never loses sight of the fact that security is a people issue. It is ultimately people who are the perpetrators and victims of business espionage; and managing people requires far more care and imagination than managing data.

Successful countermeasures managers need to look carefully at the people they work with and ask themselves some difficult questions:

1. What suspicious activities have individual employees and associates performed?
2. What reasons might individual employees and associates have for initiating acts of espionage?
3. What factors might make individual employees and associates susceptible to being recruited for espionage?
4. How aware are individual employees and associates of their security-related risks and responsibilities?
5. What security-related measures will motivate individual employees and associates to be safer, happier, and more productive?

Perhaps the toughest question to answer is the last one. Managers may feel they have done their duty by establishing, announcing, monitoring, and enforcing security policies. In fact, their role also extends to motivating and inspiring. Unless company employees are inspired to assume security responsibilities on their own, the system as a whole collapses.

In most cases, a manager can motivate employees to take a more personal stake in preventing business espionage by holding open discussions: The manager can outline, thoughtfully and constructively, the potential espionage risk in an employee's particular area as well as the potential consequences of espionage to that employee's productivity and career. This approach gives employees much more information about security risks in their areas of responsibility than they could ever learn on their own. Ideally, such discussions are held at regular intervals to encourage ongoing alertness to espionage issues. The discussions can even be incorporated into performance appraisals.

In companies where institutional loyalty or job identification is more tenuous, the concept of security needs to be presented in a more engaging way. One corporate head of security in a retail company called in Questor Group consultants just before her annual "holiday horror" briefing to the sales force. In earlier years, her talk and printed backup materials had focused exclusively on how to keep the store from being ripped off. The consultants recommended a different approach for the upcoming briefing, one that would consistently link the "store family" with the "home family." For example, *The Basic Security Tip Sheet*, distributed to all full-time and part-time employees at the briefing, was rewritten so that it expressed security measures in everyday language that could be applied to both the store and the home:

1. Keep the interior and all entrances well lighted.
2. Don't provide places for thieves or spies to hide.
3. Keep doors locked or on door alarms when not in use.
4. Check to see that alarms are working properly.
5. Avoid routine procedures that can be observed and exploited by thieves or spies.
6. Call for help if you feel threatened.
7. Keep cash and other valuables at the lowest possible levels.
8. Go directly to the bank when making bank deposits.
9. Do not leave bank deposits, valuables, or important documents unattended.
10. Report loiterers or other suspicious people.
11. Write down license numbers and descriptions of suspicious vehicles.
12. Take no action that would jeopardize your personal safety.

The security officer's preholiday briefing changed from just another pep talk to something that employees could relate to their personal lives. Throughout the "open mike" discussion of security issues, the officer drew strong parallels between the safeguards necessary to reduce security risks at home and those required to reduce risks in business. It became clearer to everyone that the store family fed the one at home and that both needed extra care.

A friendly, equitable working environment is clearly the best insurance against homegrown spies. Even so, people-oriented countermeasures managers are not just nice, caring advisers. They are also diligent investigators, especially at the very beginning of the employer-employee relationship—the hiring process itself. It is amazing how lax human resources departments and managers can be about conducting background checks on all potential employees and temporary workers.

In a 1985 survey of leading U.S. business executives conducted by *Security World* magazine, 25 percent of the respondents admitted that their firms had unknowingly hired management-level employees on the strength of bogus résumés. One retired executive, a man who had held a number of responsible positions both in and out of government, actually bragged to his friends about his ability to commit this type of fraud. Early in his career, he claimed to have researched private colleges that had gone out of business. When he found a school that no longer had records available, he would use its name on a résumé. "I needn't have bothered," he added. "No one ever checked as far as I know." A conscientious manager would have checked and would have requested personal documents to verify an applicant's professed college credentials.

Simply as a matter of legal protection, new employees should be asked to sign an agreement to protect the confidentiality of the company's trade secrets. During exit interviews, departing employees should be reminded of this agreement. A countermeasures manager can make further use of the exit interview by skillful probing: How does a departing employee feel about security policies and procedures? Does the departing employee have resentments, ambitions, or resources that could lead to later espionage against a company employee, a company department, or the company as a whole?

A countermeasures manager, working independently and with human resources personnel, should also check out prospective consultants who are brought in for project assignments. Outside experts who have access to inside information are always a threat, especially the "instant experts" who pop up to capitalize on a new fad or trend. It's equally important for a manager to examine the full-time staff's freelance work, consulting jobs, or second businesses. Employees should never initiate independent business relationships with their company's competitors or vendors: Even if the employees take pains to prevent an outright conflict of interest, they remain highly exposed targets for business spies.

TAKING STOCK OF SECURITY RISKS

As headlined in Chapter 2, Yukichi Fukuzawa, samurai founder of Keio University in Japan, once observed: "The present world can be designated as one of business and war." To help set security goals and catalog what they need to achieve those goals, business managers can benefit from this slogan:

> Declare **WAR** on Business Espionage!
> **W**—What are my objectives?
> **A**— Actions to be taken?
> **R**— Results expected?

In security matters, as in any other facet of business operations, the more specific and measurable goals are, the more effectively they can be implemented, and the more impressive the results will be. Before countermeasures managers can define specific and measurable security goals, or successfully cooperate with professional security investigators, they need to do some purely exploratory legwork, eyework, and mindwork. They must go beyond their regular routines and survey their physical surroundings in a whole new way. It helps if they behave a little like spies themselves.

Here is a "security walkthrough" model that is adaptable to any business environment. Assume that your executive or managerial responsibilities put you in charge of a small office building or plant. On your next trip to the office, drive a different vehicle, take a different route, park a different place, and/or use a different entrance. Breaking your own routine will help you adopt a different point of view. You'll also be more likely to observe people when they are off their guard.

Human awareness is keyed to color, form, and use. Change these three, or change their emphasis or configuration, and perception changes as well. As you make your security rounds, drive a gray wagon instead of your usual blue sedan, wear a checkered stadium coat instead of your usual wool herringbone, don a hat if you seldom wear one—suddenly you'll no longer look like The Boss. One top executive keeps an old sweater and some small bags of potato chips in the trunk of her car. No one looks official wearing a baggy sweater and munching chips.

Approach your facility by a different route. Use the back road near the tracks or the alley next to the repair shop. Are there holes in the fence, pathways through the grass, out-of-the-way hiding places? Is there a new lock on the back gate? A favorite trick of thieves and spies is to cut the padlock off a little-used gate and install another of the same make. They then have a private entrance.

Park as close to the least-used entrance as you can and look around. Who else parks there? Why? Check all possible hiding places near the entrance where stolen items could be concealed for later pickup. Look behind freestanding walls, clumps of foliage, and piles of material or refuse. Lift the plastic liner out of each trash container and see what's stashed between the liner and the bottom of the can. Take a quick peek under the sink in the janitor's closet. Push up the overhead panel in the nearest elevator and inspect the space within: To thieves and spies, an elevator is a private room between floors.

Most important, fight the feeling that you are being overly suspicious and melodramatic. You aren't. Here is a partial list of stolen items that have literally been spotted going out of companies through elevators, doors, gates, and other points: roll film, film plates, photocopies, computer records, truck engines, septic tanks, blueprints, weapons, precious metals, paint, stereo records, chemicals, canned food, clothing, furs, bags of cement, a cabin cruiser with trailer, electronics equipment, antique furniture, fresh fish, and mud samples from a drilling rig on Alaska's North Slope.

THE AFTER-HOURS SECURITY TOUR

An after-hours walkthrough can be even more revealing. You may discover a different company, a different world, if you leave the premises for the day as usual and then come back an hour or two later. Again, it helps to think like a spy. Take along a flashlight and a pocket mirror, so that you can gain visibility above, below, and behind objects. Carry a pocket tape recorder to make on-the-spot notes as quickly and efficiently as possible.

While waiting for the company to shift from "nine to five" to "after hours," tour the surrounding community. No company, no matter how large, is a world unto itself. You may find it a shock, for example, to discover that a storefront four blocks away is local headquarters for a militant group or that street people live under the highway exit ramp that your employees use. Militants or street people may pose no threat, but it is better to know they are there than not to know.

A nearby key shop may advertise that it makes duplicate keys of a type you once thought were secure. One neighborhood key shop owner told an official from a large private research institution, "We make all the special keys for you guys." When the official asked the shop owner how he became an authorized dealer for that particular line of security keys and locks, the shop owner explained, "Your people kept asking us to make duplicate keys. We didn't have the key blanks so we had to add that line to the others we carry."

A tour of local pawnshops, used-goods stores, and garage sales may indicate that company controls need tightening up. Consultants now with The Questor Group once went to a large garage sale only a few blocks away from a client firm. Component parts were lined up on a shelf as they would have been in the company stockroom. The consultants told the sale organizer, a company employee, that they were fellow workers and asked him if he wasn't worried that a company executive might show up. He scoffed, "Everyone lives in the suburbs. None of the brass would come down here."

Although this display of parts involved theft rather than espionage, it pointed to a poor security system that could benefit both spies and thieves. Moreover, a garage sale offering stolen goods is a valuable source of information for business spies. Questions like "Where can I get product Z from the company?" and "What's the dirt on Mr. K, who runs the computer section?" don't seem out of place when a spy has just purchased several hundred dollars' worth of stolen merchandise.

Once you have surveyed the neighborhood, return to the company, again driving a different car, taking a different route, and/or using a different entrance. Begin by checking the keys that security guards carry on their key rings. Master keys are distributed much more widely than they are supposed to be, and than most companies would suspect. Night supervisors often find key control so complicated that they simply give out master keys to everyone on their shift. Continue to check for unauthorized master keys as you make your rounds. At the same time, try to view everything you pass with fresh eyes. Look, in particular, for exceptions, oddities, and irregularities.

Exceptions

Note employees still on the premises who are in areas of the company not associated with their regular work (especially employees with special keys or special privileges).

Give close attention to all possible points of entry to the premises: doors, windows, skylights, vents. Entry points that have been left open or unguarded should be considered dangerous. Ask yourself: "Why is this particular vent uncovered?" "Whose car is parked just outside this open window?"

Oddities

Identify any computers (especially personal computers) capable of running communications, data-sorting, or other software programs that are not normally used in a particular part of the business. Any software program that is not supplied by the company, and thus not controlled by its computer security systems, should be suspect. Give close scrutiny to any papers lying around that describe access to outside computer bulletin boards or contain computer "hacker" information. These papers can indicate potential computer theft problems just as drug paraphernalia can indicate drug use problems. One private investigator tried to log onto a computer bulletin board he found listed in a client's computer room. The bulletin board was for hackers and was open only to newcomers who supplied other access codes as "dues" when they joined.

If computer equipment is running, check what is coming in and going out. It could be company business, private business, or spy work. Examine any personal music systems, intercoms, or other electronic devices brought onto the premises by company personnel. Look closely for modifications that suggest eavesdropping.

Irregularities

Be suspicious if truckers, creditors, or others show up and ask to deal with a specific employee and no one else. Illegal deals are most frequently consummated after hours.

Check to see that guards are making their prescribed rounds. In one undercover investigation at a major manufacturing outfit, agents put a drop of clear cement and a thumbprint on the head of each screw that held a guard key in place at the various checkpoints around the company. The guard was supposed to visit each of these stations once an hour and use the key to punch the guard clock he carried. Discovering one morning that the thumbprint on each key screw had been pierced, the agents figured out that the guard had removed the screws on his first round and had brought them to his desk, where he had remained for the rest of the evening, punching the guard clock each hour without making his rounds.

Pick up telephones that ring. Late-night calls can often signal out-of-the-ordinary practices. An investigation of after-hours calls at one construction supply firm revealed that a sales representative had been conducting a second, clandestine business on the premises.

In addition to keeping an eye out for miscellaneous exceptions, oddities, and irregularities, take a closer look at features of the physical environment that initially show no suspicious signs. Here are some suggestions.

Bulletin Boards

Check the notices advertising outside activities, such as computer and photography clubs. You may want to do some investigation into the nature of these organizations, especially if you've never heard of them before.

During a routine assignment for a chemicals laboratory, an undercover agent was invited by a fellow employee to join a local photography club. The employee was primarily interested in commercial photography, as were several club members from other firms. Informal exhibitions of members' work often revealed exciting—and confidential—information about what was happening at the club members' companies. One exhibit featured color close-ups of a restricted-access project: exotic ice crystals forming in a chemical broth. The photographer saw the pictures as art. The agent saw them as potentially dangerous information leaks.

Lighting

Pay careful attention to poorly lit areas inside and outside the building: They can conceal spies, spy equipment, or company materials en route to spy clients. One simple way to test for poor lighting is to try reading the column headings of a newspaper in the lighted area.

The Mail Room

Any site where mail is processed in or out should be of as much interest to countermeasures managers as it is to corporate spies. What items are lying about a mail room that belong under lock and key? Blueprints to be discussed at tomorrow's meeting, the latest bids from Chicago, even ordinary items like company stationery and order forms can easily put a spy in business.

The Copy Center

Look for blank forms, documents left over from the day, and papers stacked to be copied tomorrow. Think about how these papers could be used by a spy. Copy center workers sometimes make extra copies of executive résumés and other items for their personal use. At the copy center in one large communications firm, trading such "extras" was a valued social activity, a form of bonding between the relatively remote copy center and other company departments. Résumés, organizational charts, and RIF (reduction in force) lists circulated freely in spite of company prohibitions.

File and Record Rooms

File rooms deserve especially careful investigation. Often they are "dead zones" that are left unattended at least part of the time. They are locked and forgotten. One manager of a software production company, conducting an informal security walk through her offices, discovered that a stranger had been living in a file room for some time! The secret resident had apparently sawed through the bolts on a security window and used it as a doorway to the alley. Once inside, the interloper dropped new bolts in place until he was ready to leave.

The Accounting Office

You do not have to be an accountant to spot information leaks in an accounting office. Most spies are not accountants either. They just make copies of everything in sight and let their clients figure things out. The slogan on a T-shirt advertised in *Soldier of Fortune*, a magazine chock-full of information for those in the spy business, sums up the philosophy well: "Kill them all! Let God sort them out!" Make sure that all papers in the accounting office are kept out of sight and preferably locked up after hours.

Shipping and Receiving Areas

Books have been written about the security problems that plague shipping and receiving areas. These books usually deal with employee theft rather than business espionage, but the two go hand in glove. The point is worth restating: There is no way of knowing how many thefts ultimately serve, or mask, spy missions. During a security walk through a shipping and receiving area, always check for:

- Loiterers (employees on shift, early birds, latecomers, relatives of employees, truck drivers, or just plain outsiders).
- Unauthorized vehicles parked nearby.
- Missing documentation and/or authorization stamps.
- Missing pages from logbooks.
- Unusual signs of packaging and repackaging on loading docks.
- Broken seals and open, unattended vehicles.
- Hand tools, ladders, and other "unusual" items stashed outside.
- Hidden areas, such as behind stacked goods.

Storage Areas

Every company has at least one storage area, on site or off, that has not been checked lately. Security analysts call them "oh yeah" areas, as in "Oh yeah, I forgot about that!" Storage areas that can be easily perceived as neglected, especially those away from the main part of the company, are particularly vulnerable to becoming "field headquarters" for spies.

Refuse Containers

Refuse containers are notoriously rich mines for business spies. Again, spies do not just want printed information; they also thrive on clean, blank pages. One security check of an off-site security vault revealed that anyone could gain access with nothing more than a note of authorization on company stationery.

Nor do spies seek only paper materials. One manufacturing plant produced mounds of metal shavings as scrap. Most of the shavings were hauled outside to a railroad car on a siding, except for those produced in an area where machinists worked on special projects—projects that kept the company on the leading edge of the industry. Clean-up people shoveled the shavings from this area into metal drums and kept them in a separate outside location, since they had greater value as scrap.

One evening as an undercover agent was leaving the special project area with the rest of his crew, a machinist who worked in a different part of the plant stopped by the barrels of expensive waste and remarked, "I see they're just about finished with part X." The agent asked him how he knew, and he said, "I see the special stock come in like everyone else. I have a rough idea what they're working on and how long it takes to make this quantity of shavings on the type of lathe they have." He went on to state that most machinists can tell the type of stock turned, its alloy composition, and the kind of cutting tools and lathes used merely by looking closely at the shavings with the naked eye—and sniffing with the naked nose!

This hypothetical security walkthrough should give you a good working sense of how, literally, to inspect a physical business environment for possible security hazards. It does not represent a full-scale professional security survey, or any type of formal security survey at all. It is simply a first-step approach to learning to see your work environment differently—the way a security analyst, or a spy, might see it.

It is a good idea to conduct these surveys regularly at every location where business spies may operate against you: at home, at the office, and at the factory. The checklists in Chapter 6 will help you arrive at a comprehensive evaluation of these three environments.

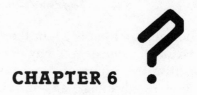

CHAPTER 6

Do It Yourself:

Security Survey Checklists and Guidelines

> "Leave the beaten track occa-
> sionally and dive into the woods.
> You will be certain to find
> something you have never seen
> before."
> **Alexander Graham Bell**

Here's the cardinal rule for being a successful leader: *Manage* tasks, don't *do* them. Business espionage, however, doesn't go by the rules. It has grown to monstrous propor-

tions in today's corporate world precisely because most managers will never get physically involved in checking it out. Unless you break management tradition and perform some fieldwork on your own, you will never develop a sixth sense for how, where, or when espionage may strike your company and cripple your productivity.

The goal of a do-it-yourself security survey is to increase your knowledge base so that you can make more effective plans and decisions. A do-it-yourself survey is not necessarily meant to result in your catching spies in action or determining which locks can be easily picked, although such results may indeed occur. Instead, it is a mission to test your own sensitivity to possible risks, threats, and irregularities in your working environments. How well do you understand the physical settings in which you, your colleagues, and your subordinates operate? How accurately can you assess the danger of espionage in these areas? How might someone commit espionage against you, right under your nose?

The best way to begin answering these questions satisfactorily is through do-it-yourself surveys. They will reveal to you what you do and don't know about the safety and efficiency of your home, factory, or office. You may not be able to match the technical expertise of a professional security investigator, but you will have an insider's advantage: an appreciation for how things are supposed to happen and a vested interest in seeing that they happen that way. What you learn through a do-it-yourself survey—and you are bound to learn *many* things—will benefit you and the people who depend on you. It will also give you an enormous head start in the event that you choose to seek the help of professionals.

The checklists that follow are based partly on my own investigative experiences and partly on the experiences of clients who were wise enough to conduct do-it-yourself surveys prior to retaining my services. Before you survey your home, factory, and/or office facility, review these checklists carefully and customize individual questions to suit your specific situation.

HOME SECURITY CHECKLIST

Yard and Grounds

Yes No

☐ ☐   1. Is shrubbery that might provide a hiding place for intruders trimmed back?

☐ ☐   2. Are trellises and other plant supports on or near the house strong enough to hold plants, but not to climb?

☐ ☐   3. Is outside lighting bright enough to read the headlines of a newspaper at night (at least near entrances and first-floor windows)?

☐ ☐   4. Do entrance fixtures have double sockets and double bulbs so that you are not in total darkness if a bulb burns out?

☐ ☐   5. Do you plan ahead so you won't have to hide a key?
Hiding keys is no protection against burglars or thieves. Criminals know all the secret places.

☐ ☐   6. Do you remove the keys and lock your vehicles even in your driveway or garage?

Yes   No

☐   ☐   7. Do you keep your garage locked even when you are at home?

Doors

☐   ☐   1. Are your doors fitted with dead-bolt locks?
To check a lock, open the door and turn the lock as if the door were closed. Then try to push the bolt back with your thumb. A dead bolt cannot be pushed back. A live bolt will push back against a spring—just as it would if the door were closed and someone pushed against the bolt with a credit card or a screwdriver. You don't want live-bolt locks.

☐   ☐   2. Do you have double-cylinder locks on doors with glass panels or on any other surface an intruder could easily penetrate?
Double-cylinder locks, which can be locked with a key from either side, are not as easy to open as regular, button-operated locks.

☐   ☐   3. Do you keep your outside doors locked at all times, even when you are on the premises?

☐   ☐   4. Did you have the locks changed when you moved into your present house or apartment?

☐   ☐   5. Do you have strong chains on all your outer doors?
The best door chains have a 3-inch lag screw that goes into the door frame and a steel loop that drops over the inside knob.

☐   ☐   6. Are your outer doors of solid construction, rather than hollow-core?
Doors can be strengthened with plywood paneling or replaced with modern metal security doors that look like wood. Decorative grillwork is also available.

Yes   No

☐ ☐   7. Do you use your door chains every time you answer the door, even when you think you know who is there?

☐ ☐   8. Do you lock up when you leave, even if you will be gone only a short time?

☐ ☐   9. Do you have peepholes in your outer doors and do you use them at all times?

☐ ☐   10. Do your basement doors have locks that allow you to cut off that part of the house, if necessary?

Windows

☐ ☐   1. Do you have bars or grillwork over windows that are easily accessible to burglars?
Do not trap yourself in case of fire. Bars or grillwork should be hinged, and locked from the inside with the key readily available but out of sight of the window. This protective measure is especially important for out-of-the-way windows favored by burglars and spies.

☐ ☐   2. Do you have adequate locks on all your windows?

☐ ☐   3. Do you lock all the windows when you go out?

☐ ☐   4. Are you as careful of second-story and basement windows as you are of those on the first floor?

☐ ☐   5. Do you chain and padlock ladders left outside so that someone cannot use them to climb in your windows or bug your house?

Keys

☐ ☐   1. Have you removed all personal identification from your keys and key cases so that if they are lost a thief will not know where to go?

☐ ☐   2. Do you always separate your house keys from your car keys when you must leave your car keys with a parking attendant or repair shop?

Yes   No

☐ ☐   3. When you lose your keys, do you always have your locks changed or rekeyed at once?

☐ ☐   4. Have you made sure that no one has a key to your house who no longer needs it (e.g., former owners, former cleaning people, realtors)?

☐ ☐   5. Do you avoid "telegraphing" your intentions in advance (e.g., taking out your car or house keys way before using them)?
        "Telegraphing" makes it easy for muggers and spies to anticipate your moves and make countermoves of their own. Spies can also identify key makes and types at a distance, if they are given enough time. Know where your keys are ahead of time so that you can reach them quickly and easily at the moment they are needed.

Safe Practices

☐ ☐   1. When you go on a trip, do you set a timer to switch your house lights and/or radio on and off at strategic hours, to give the impression someone is home?

☐ ☐   2. Do you keep your travel plans secret, except from reliable friends and associates on a need-to-know basis?

☐ ☐   3. When you are away, do you arrange to have newspapers, mail, and other deliveries either stopped or picked up daily by a reliable friend?

☐ ☐   4. Do you keep large amounts of money or other valuables in the bank or in a safety-deposit box, where they should be, instead of at home?

☐ ☐   5. Do you make certain that it is *not* common knowledge that you have a safe or vault at home? If you have a safe or vault in your home, don't advertise the fact, and be sure the company that installed it doesn't list you as a reference for its services.

☐ ☐   6. Do you keep an inventory of valuables and inscribe your driver's license or other code number on valuable items?

☐ ☐   7. Are your checkbooks and credit cards kept under lock and key?

☐ ☐   8. Do you check the identification of repairpeople and other strangers before you allow them to enter your home?
Always check a stranger's identification by calling the company that the stranger claims to represent. Do not use the telephone number that the visitor gives you. Call the number in the telephone directory or the one provided by directory assistance.

☐ ☐   9. Are you alert to strangers loitering in the neighborhood?

☐ ☐   10. Do you jot down license numbers of suspicious vehicles?

☐ ☐   11. Do you have police and fire department numbers posted by every phone?

OFFICE SECURITY CHECKLIST

Perimeter Areas

☐ ☐   1. Is shrubbery that might provide a hiding place for intruders trimmed back?

☐ ☐   2. Have you looked at the areas on all six sides of the office (north, south, east, west, above, and below) for security hazards presented by neighboring facilities?

☐ ☐   3. Is outside lighting bright enough to read the headlines of a newspaper at night (at least near entrances and first-floor windows)?

Yes   *No*

☐   ☐   4. Is someone available to replace burned-out light bulbs, and do you know how to contact that person even if you are working alone at night or on weekends?

☐   ☐   5. Do you plan ahead so that you won't have to hide a key or key card?

☐   ☐   6. Do appropriate safeguards guarantee that ventilators, elevator houses, and stairwells do *not* offer easy access to the building after hours?

☐   ☐   7. Do you make certain to lock up valuable data and materials along the access routes most likely to be used by thieves or spies as they enter and leave the office?

☐   ☐   8. Do you know the history of criminal activity (reported burglaries, assaults, and so on) for your office building and do you use this history to spot potential weaknesses in your own security?
Contact the local police and security services for information on past crimes. It can be a powerful tool in convincing building management to make needed changes.

☐   ☐   9. Do you encourage vigilance in other employees, including maintenance personnel?

☐   ☐   10. Do you have police and fire department telephone numbers posted by every phone?

Doors

☐   ☐   1. Are your office doors fitted with dead-bolt locks?

☐   ☐   2. Do you have double-cylinder locks on doors with glass panels or on any other surface an intruder could easily penetrate?

☐   ☐   3. Are office doors of solid construction rather than hollow-core?

Yes *No*

Keys

☐ ☐ 1. Have you removed all identification from your keys and key cases so that if they are lost a thief will not know where to go?

☐ ☐ 2. Do you always separate your house and office keys from your car keys when you must leave your car keys with a parking attendant or repair shop?

☐ ☐ 3. When you lose your keys, do you always have your locks changed or rekeyed at once?

☐ ☐ 4. Have you made sure that there are no people who possess a key to your office if they no longer need one (e.g., former employees, reassigned cleaning people)?

☐ ☐ 5. Do you avoid "telegraphing" your intentions in advance (e.g., taking out your car or office keys way before using them)?

☐ ☐ 6. Do you have a key control system that everyone in the office understands and uses?
A key control system can be as simple as a sign-out sheet kept up to date by the office manager or as complex as a customized computer tracking program.

☐ ☐ 7. Was the locking system (locks, lock cylinders, key cards, or other devices) changed when you moved into the office?

☐ ☐ 8. When the office is open for business, do you control access to important rooms with electric door latches, buzzers, or other control devices?

Windows

☐ ☐ 1. Do you have bars or grillwork over windows that are easily accessible to burglars?

☐ ☐ 2. Do you have adequate locks on all your windows?

Yes No

☐ ☐   3. Are all windows locked when no one is on the premises?

☐ ☐   4. Are basement and upper-story windows as carefully secured as first-floor windows?

☐ ☐   5. In high-rise buildings, are windows onto balconies and public access areas carefully secured?

Intrusion Detection Devices

☐ ☐   1. Do you understand the intrusion detection devices (burglar and other alarms) in the office and know how to test them?

☐ ☐   2. Do you know whom to call, even after hours, if the alarms do not work as they should?

☐ ☐   3. Do you lock up and set the alarms when you leave, even if you will be gone only a short time? Spies and other thieves frequently gain unobserved access to offices by having solitary workers called to the lobby to "pick up a package."

Employee Identification

☐ ☐   1. Do you have an employee identification program, including visitors' passes, that everyone in the office understands and uses?
Even small companies need visitor escorts and visitor's passes if critical data and materials are present. In companies so large that individual employees do not know all other employees by sight, every employee should wear a visible ID tag for complete security.

☐ ☐   2. Do you check the identification of repairpeople, salespeople, and other strangers before you allow them to enter the office?

☐ ☐   3. Are janitors, building contractors, vendors, and repairpeople issued passes and confined to the areas they need to occupy?

Yes No

□ □ 4. Are important materials locked away while workers or other visitors are in critical areas?

Company Records

□ □ 1. Are critical company papers, computer tapes, blueprints, plans, and models given special protection?

□ □ 2. Do you have a document classification system that everyone in the office understands and uses?
A classification system need not involve stamping papers SECRET and following government standards for document control—unless that level of security is advisable. A safe with a checkout system for critical items may be sufficient. Initialing the upper-right-hand corner of a document is a simple way of marking it for special treatment.

□ □ 3. Do you log important items in and out so that someone is always responsible for them?
For a free look at a basic document control system, talk to the librarian in charge of the rare book collection at the public library.

□ □ 4. Do you keep copies of important records at a secure facility away from the office?

□ □ 5. Do you review information control procedures at least once a month and carefully check any irregularities?

Money and Other Valuables

□ □ 1. Do you keep large amounts of money or other valuables in the bank or in a safety-deposit box, where they should be, instead of at the office?

□ □ 2. Do you make certain that it is *not* common knowledge that you keep large amounts of money or other valuables at the office?

To change your image of vulnerability, you may want to start using an armored car service or at least post signs that indicate you don't keep cash on hand.

☐ ☐ 3. Do you keep an inventory of valuables, including office equipment, in a safe, separate location and inscribe your driver's license or other code number on valuable items?

Mail

☐ ☐ 1. Does your mail pass through unauthorized hands on its way to you?

☐ ☐ 2. Is mail left in the hall or in unlocked mail rooms?

☐ ☐ 3. Are the date and time stamped on each piece of mail as it arrives on the premises to establish accountability?

Company Vehicles

☐ ☐ 1. Are company vehicles kept locked, even while in the company parking lot?

☐ ☐ 2. Do you make sure that you do *not* leave sales records, blueprints, computer disks, or other important items unattended in a company vehicle (or any other vehicle, for that matter), even when it is locked?

FACTORY SECURITY CHECKLIST

Surrounding Neighborhood

Yes   *No*

☐ ☐ 1. Have you given full consideration to any special security problems presented by the local terrain?

A river or lake adjacent to the plant may be more like a roadway than a barrier. A hill, even one at some distance, may be an observation post for spies or other thieves.

☐ ☐   2. Have you given full consideration to any possible threats posed by neighboring facilities or organizations?

☐ ☐   3. Are there neighborhood organizations you should become more active in for security reasons?

☐ ☐   4. Do you know the history of criminal activity (reported burglaries, assaults, and so on) in your area and do you use this information to spot potential weaknesses in your own security?

Factory Perimeter

☐ ☐   1. Is shrubbery that might provide a hiding place for intruders trimmed back?

☐ ☐   2. Have you looked at the areas on all six sides of the plant (north, south, east, west, above, and below) for possible security hazards?

☐ ☐   3. Is outside lighting all around the perimeter bright enough to read newspaper headlines at night?

☐ ☐   4. Do you have an emergency lighting system that will take over if the regular lighting fails?

☐ ☐   5. Do you know how the backup lighting system works and how to test it?

☐ ☐   6. Is someone available to replace burned-out lights on evenings and weekends and do you know how to contact that person?

Fences

☐ ☐   1. Are existing fences best suited to the terrain and history of criminal activity in the area?

Yes   No

☐   ☐   2. Are the fences high enough to counteract the potential threat?

☐   ☐   3. Are the fences far enough from buildings that they cannot be easily bridged with standard lumber?

☐   ☐   4. Are the areas along both sides of the fences cleared, so that any holes or gaps can be easily detected?

☐   ☐   5. Is the fencing straight (i.e., can you sight down the fence line in both directions)?
Out-of-plumb fence posts and bulges in the fencing fabric may be signs that the fence has been cut along the lower edge or breached in some other manner. The same is true of sags in lines of barbed wire.

☐   ☐   6. Are security patrols laid out so that guards can sight along fence lines and physically examine the fences?

☐   ☐   7. If tension sensors or other intrusion alarms are connected to the fences, do you know how to test them?

☐   ☐   8. Do you know whom to contact, even on weekends or holidays, if the alarm system doesn't work?

Gates

☐   ☐   1. Are all gates properly hung so that they cannot be lifted off their hinges?
Some wire-mesh gates are hung on hinge pins clamped to upright metal posts. The clamps can be removed with a socket wrench and the gate can then be lifted off or swung aside.

☐   ☐   2. Are the padlocks on little-used gates checked frequently?
Padlocks should have permanent identification numbers and be checked regularly with the key that is supposed to open them.

Yes No

□ □ 3. Have you made sure that there are no unusual signs of traffic near little-used gates?

□ □ 4. Do you plan ahead so that you won't have to leave a key or key card near a gate or other entrance?

Parking Areas

□ □ 1. Have you made sure that there are no cars or other vehicles parked near interior fences?

□ □ 2. Have you made sure there are no signs of unauthorized foot traffic between sensitive areas of the plant and the parking lot(s)?

□ □ 3. Have you made sure that visitors' cars are not allowed inside the perimeter fence?

□ □ 4. Are security guards involved in traffic control?

Key Control

□ □ 1. Is there a master key system?

□ □ 2. Are keys, especially master keys, controlled with the same level of security as the materials and information they safeguard?

□ □ 3. Are vital company records and materials on a separate control system?
High-tech card key or other electronic locking systems are useful for critical areas. They can tell you who unlocked what and when.

□ □ 4. Are key cabinets kept locked when not in use?

□ □ 5. Are key supplies (key blanks, lock cores, and so on) locked up separately and controlled as carefully as the keys themselves?

□ □ 6. Are keys inventoried regularly?

□ □ 7. Is each employee accountable for his or her own keys?

Yes *No*

Cash and Cashables

☐ ☐ 1. Do you make sure that you don't keep more cash or cashables on the premises than necessary?

☐ ☐ 2. Do you deposit cash or cashables frequently enough for them to be safe?
Consider also whether you should send company records to a record bank or any other off-site depository more frequently in order to make them safer.

☐ ☐ 3. Are protective measures taken to safeguard valuables in transit?
One of the most effective security measures is to change the route of transit. The first and last few hundred yards on the transit route are the most dangerous because they are the most difficult to vary.

☐ ☐ 4. Would an armored car company or professional courier service help make your deposit system safer?

Security Guards

☐ ☐ 1. Are security guard duties reviewed on a regular basis?
Important changes in the company should be reflected by changes in the security department. Security department routines should be updated whenever new buildings, new equipment, or new business functions are added.

☐ ☐ 2. Does guard training include briefings on business espionage controls and countermeasures?
If, for example, new computers are installed at the plant, security guards need to know who is authorized to use them and how the system operates so they can tell when company guidelines are being violated.

Yes   No

☐   ☐   3. Are guard schedules arranged to give good coverage during shift changes and breaks?

☐   ☐   4. Do security guard patrols cover all important areas, especially those on the perimeter?

☐   ☐   5. Do guard training manuals reflect the latest company policies and procedures?

☐   ☐   6. Are there written instructions for each guard post and patrol?

☐   ☐   7. Are guard reports and the reporting system adequate?
A three-part ticket, printed in house, is a simple and effective reporting system. When a door is found unlocked or some other discrepancy is noted, the guard completes the ticket. One copy is left on the supervisor's desk in the department where the discrepancy occurs, one goes to the security office, and one is kept by the guard.

☐   ☐   8. If you use a contract guard service, is it retained mainly because of expertise rather than low price?
Expect to pay more for contract guards with high-quality training and equipment—the kind most companies need.

☐   ☐   9. Are armed security guards given special training?
Under most circumstances, security guards should not be armed. (Arms include nightsticks, knockdown sprays, and personal weapons.) If armed, guards should have special training in all the legal implications of carrying and using arms.

Warehouses, Loading Docks, and Outdoor Storage Areas

☐   ☐   1. Are there written procedures to ensure accountability for all company property?

☐   ☐   2. Are route slips and other records (including computer records) "working documents" that can be

Yes   No

used to track parts and products through the plant and establish accountability?

☐ ☐ 3. Are delivery personnel confined to the loading dock or other controlled areas?

☐ ☐ 4. Are delivery records checked against purchase orders and these in turn checked against actual merchandise?

☐ ☐ 5. Are unauthorized personnel kept out of storage areas?

☐ ☐ 6. Are important storage areas closed to outside observation?

☐ ☐ 7. Is there a separate cage or "safe room" for valuable merchandise, cases that have been broken open, and important records in transit?

☐ ☐ 8. Is material in open storage stacked away from fences so that the fence lines remain visible and areas close to the fences can be patrolled?
Unscrupulous employees or intruders can easily get away with dumping material over a fence if the material is stored close by.

Production Lines

☐ ☐ 1. Are there written guidelines for production shutdown and lockup procedures?

☐ ☐ 2. Have you made sure that ventilators, elevator houses, and stairwells do *not* offer easy afterhours access to production areas?

☐ ☐ 3. Have you made certain that it is *not* possible to gain access to office and other plant facilities along production lines or openings cut for conveyors?

☐ ☐ 4. Do you make certain to lock up valuable data and materials along the access routes most likely to be used by thieves as they enter and leave the factory?

☐ ☐ 5. Do you encourage vigilance in other employees, including maintenance personnel?

Yes   *No*

☐   ☐   6. Do you have police and fire department numbers posted by every phone?

Interior Doors and Locks

☐   ☐   1. Are important interior doors fitted with dead-bolt or other secure locks?

☐   ☐   2. Do you have double-cylinder locks on doors with glass panels or on other surfaces that an intruder could easily penetrate?

☐   ☐   3. Are plan rooms, tool rooms, and other important factory centers behind solid-core doors?

☐   ☐   4. Are there written guidelines concerning safeguards for employee lockers, desks, and other private areas?

Interior Traffic Control

☐   ☐   1. Are factory areas "zoned" on a need-to-know and a need-to-be-there basis?

☐   ☐   2. Do you have an employee identification program that remains in effect inside the plant?
The identification card for getting through the front gate can also be used as a clip-on pass within the company. The card can be "zoned" using a color, letter, or number code, or a combination of the three.

☐   ☐   3. Do you check the identification of repairpeople, salespeople, and other strangers before you allow them to enter the plant?

☐   ☐   4. Do you have a document classification system that everyone at the plant understands and uses?

☐   ☐   5. Do you log important items in and out so that someone is always responsible for them?

☐   ☐   6. Do you keep copies of important records at a secure facility away from the plant?

☐ ☐ 7. Do you review information control procedures at least once a month and carefully check out any irregularities?

Interior Electrical Control and Robotic Devices

☐ ☐ 1. Do you know how to lock up, lock out, and lock off controls on electrical panels and other control devices?

☐ ☐ 2. Do you know whom to call, even after hours, if someone has forgotten to lock up, lock out, or lock off?

☐ ☐ 3. Are robots and robotic devices locked off when not in authorized use?

Vehicles

☐ ☐ 1. Are electric cars and other vehicles that are used inside the plant kept locked when not signed out to someone or otherwise accounted for?

☐ ☐ 2. Are vehicles kept locked when the driver is away?

☐ ☐ 3. Do you make sure that sales records, blueprints, computer disks, or other important items are *not* left unattended in vehicles, even when the vehicles are locked?

Through talks, brochures, and newsletters, The Questor Group has shared these do-it-yourself survey checklists with many concerned managers and executives across the nation. As a result, we have developed a data file entitled "Questions We Are Asked Most Often." Understandably, almost all of these questions refer to surveys of offices and factories rather than private homes, where the surveyor has far more freedom and power to act as he or she chooses. Here are some of the key questions from our data file, and the answers we most often provide.

What Should I Wear and What Should I Take With Me When I Do a Survey of My Home or Business Facility?

We always suggest clothes that are durable and that you don't mind getting dirty. Coveralls are an excellent idea. So is a stocking cap. As my colleague Jana Pobiarzyn says, "You can't expect to do a good security survey without getting filthy dirty and meeting some creepy-crawlies face to face." A hard hat is appropriate in some spots, and there are certain areas where a hard hat is required during task performance.

The equipment you need will vary according to the facility being surveyed. Standard equipment includes a flashlight, a notebook, a pencil, a tape recorder, and graph paper for making accurate sketches and diagrams. A small, metal hand mirror helps you to see around, above, and below things, and a stepladder enables you to inspect areas you can't reach. You may want to take a Polaroid camera or a camcorder as well.

Should I Tell Someone I Am Going to Do a Survey?

We always suggest that you let someone you trust know where you are going and when. You don't want to fall down a shaft and be stranded until morning. Performing a survey is a lot like going on an expedition into unknown territory: You need a Stanley when you are Dr. Livingston.

Should I Take Anyone With Me on a Survey?

It is often wise to take someone you trust along with you, particularly if that person knows a lot about the physical layout of the area you are surveying. In some cases, it is almost a necessity to recruit an assistant if you want to do a thorough job. For example, you may require someone with training to turn equipment on and off for safe inspections or someone with muscle power to transport ladders.

What Should I Say If Someone Asks Me What I Am Doing While I Am Conducting My Survey?

Just say that you are doing a safety check. It's an accurate answer, even if it isn't a complete one. Most people react favorably to a company's effort to make the work environment less hazardous.

Should I Personally Take Care of Physical Security Problems That I Notice in the Course of the Survey?

Be very careful about intervening to correct anything that looks amiss—for instance, important papers lying in full view or open windows that should be kept locked. Stop, look, and listen first. Try to determine if what you see is only one part of a bigger problem. Thoughtful study of a desk top covered with confidential papers may reveal a spy's motive or modus operandi. A close look outside an unlocked window may reveal a suspicious vehicle parked nearby.

We often suggest that managers use a simple three-part "ticket" system when doing a survey, at least for minor infractions. An ordinary notebook and two pieces of carbon paper will suffice. The "who, what, where, and when" of each incident should be jotted down, with one copy left where the infraction occurred, one copy sent to the supervisor in charge, and one copy retained by the surveyor. Variations on this theme can be developed by the manager, who may decide not to leave a ticket where the infraction occurred until the seriousness of the incident can be reviewed.

In some instances, however, common sense dictates that you take it upon yourself to make company property secure. Lock the papers away. Close and secure the windows. Just remember that your main objectives in the survey are to *discover* and *assess* security problems, not to solve them on the spot, and that any action you take should be cautious and well considered.

After conducting do-it-yourself surveys, many managers feel confident about making changes in physical security without seeking the help of a professional consultant. For example, a manager in southeastern Alaska noticed that his company's garbage truck made pickups at garbage cans along the back side of the company's warehouse—an area that was out of sight of the security guard by the gate. By having the guardhouse moved a few feet and a stack of lumber shifted, the manager made sure that the guard had a better view of what was going on.

After her do-it-yourself survey, the office manager of a large law firm in Washington, D.C., became concerned about the safety of the firm's attractively open floor plan. Clients and other visitors could wander around freely and get lost or, worse, gain access to confidential information. She wanted to keep the openness and avoid the hassle of a pass system for visitors, but she also wanted to exercise more control over where nonemployees went. Her solution was to zone the carpeting with colors. One color helps visitors find the conference rooms and offices that are open to the public. Another color identifies a "courtesy zone" where anyone not known to the employees is automatically questioned and redirected.

What Should I Do If I Find an Electronic Bug?

Whenever someone poses this question, we have to turn around and ask our own questions to come up with an answer that works for that individual. We begin by asking, "What do you *want* to do, on the basis of what you know about your business and about who might have a reason for bugging you? Whom do you suspect? A professional spy? A competitor? A business associate? A lover?" The responses you make to these questions will help you decide whether you should avoid tampering with the bug until you know more, remove the bug at once, or let anyone in particular know that you have found the bug.

The best answer in most situations is to leave the bug in place and contact the appropriate law enforcement agency for advice. A private investigator may be able to trace the bug to the person who planted it by examining the characteristics of the device and backtracking, but the odds are against success.

In any event, most people have good reasons for not wanting to confront by themselves whoever may have planted the bug, and so they wisely enlist someone else's assistance right from the start.

For example, one discoverer of a bug performed work for the government. He knew he was required to inform that client, and when he did, he was advised to contact the FBI. Another discoverer of a bug was involved in legal action with a competitor. She called her attorney first, then the local police.

If the bug is attached to a telephone or any other piece of communications equipment, the supplier of that equipment may need to know how it was installed in order to readjust the system. Check with the individual supplier to determine its company policy. Some suppliers may simply disconnect the bug and leave you to pursue the matter further.

What Should I Do If I Witness an Employee Behaving in a Suspicious Manner?

Stop, look, and listen when you see, or think you see, an employee behaving suspiciously. Do this whether you suspect the person sees you or not. Your best spur-of-the-moment guideline is the motto of Confucius: "Follow the actions of a prudent person." It is prudent to take in the complete picture before intervening. It is prudent to watch the person's hands and anything he or she might use as a weapon. It is prudent to protect yourself at all times and to back away from a potentially dangerous situation unless you are trained to handle such circumstances.

A manager has the right to a full explanation of almost anything that happens on company time and/or on the company premises, as long as it doesn't violate the personal rights of the employee. For example, you may ask an employee to explain his bulging pockets, but you can't go through his pockets yourself.

I have observed many managers confront employees who may have been innocently negligent—first when I was working undercover myself, then when I trained and supervised undercover agents, and finally as a consultant making the rounds with managers. Most productive confrontations of this type begin like friendly question-and-answer sessions.

For instance, I once worked undercover as a laborer in a large industrial plant; since I was hot on the trail of a serious espionage problem, I was spending more time looking around and talking to my co-workers than I was performing my cover-job duties. A manager who had no idea I was an undercover agent saw me wandering into a sensitive area and followed me. He identified himself, asked for my name and employee number, and interviewed me about my cleaning assignment and my reasons for being in that area. He adopted a very direct but relaxed approach along the lines of what we now call "one minute management." He was frank, fair, and thorough, and he took notes that included the time and date.

By the end of our talk, I was comfortable enough with this manager's calm, rational manner to admit that I wasn't doing as well as I could as a scrap handler, and I promised to do better. He let me off with a friendly but no-nonsense warning: one that I could respect and that didn't cause either of us to develop hostile feelings.

In a surprise encounter with an employee, it is always best to keep your cool and avoid any irreparable damage. Pause long enough to ask yourself: "How can we *both* profit from this encounter—the employee with better work performance and increased self-esteem, and I with a better insight as to why this problem occurred and how extensive it is?" It is good policy to be cautious and constructive in any unanticipated meeting with another human being, even if that person may turn out to be a criminal!

When you are certain that the employee is stealing, snooping, or misusing company property, you must take *some* action, and the sooner, the better. To do nothing is to condone, or at least to contribute to, the employee's misbehavior, and the more you delay, the more damage will be done. In situations where a face-to-face confrontation is inappropriate or undesirable according to your own commonsense judgment, simply observe as much as you safely can and then report your observations to the employee's immediate supervisor, your boss, or the head of security.

What Should I Do If I See an Outsider Behaving in a Suspicious Manner?

Again, stop, look, and listen first. You can try to handle the situation by using the same question-and-answer strategy you would use with an employee; however, you are more likely to need immediate assistance from your security team or the police when you deal with outsiders. Because outsiders aren't worried about their jobs or what people in the company will think of them, they have fewer reasons to cooperate with you. Because they are strangers, you are left with almost no information on them should they decide to bolt.

Above all, make sure that what you see is actually a theft or a spying attempt before doing anything overt. If you act prematurely, you may put both yourself and your company on very shaky legal ground. You may also alienate someone who turns out to be an important associate or client.

A recent incident I witnessed serves as an illustration of this point. A friend of mine trains store security people for a nationwide chain of high-fashion outlets. Each salesperson who works for this chain keeps a card file on his or her customers; the file contains information about the customer's sizes and measurements as well as notations indicating which furs, styles, and brands might appeal to that customer. My friend was concerned that someone was stealing this information from one of the outlets, so I dropped by the outlet to discuss the situation with her.

While my friend and I were seated in her office, the salon manager hit the silent alarm. When we joined the manager, she was watching a woman who had just been flipping through one of the customer card files left in plain view on a desk. The woman was now out of sight behind the racks of furs. The salon manager had spotted the woman while making her rounds and had stopped, looked, and listened before taking action. It was wise of her, especially since she didn't recognize the person. Checks with other members of the staff revealed that the woman was the wealthy wife of a city official who had come in to see the latest collection. When she couldn't find the salesperson who normally helped her, she looked up her own card in the file to see if there were any new notations about things she might like.

What Should I Do If I Come Across Someone Who I Am Sure Is Guilty of Business Espionage?

Whether this individual is an employee or a stranger, you should proceed with great care so that your actions don't backfire on you or your company. Before you make any accusations, either to the suspected spy or to anyone else, you need to amass as much evidence as you can about the "who, what, why, where, when, and how" aspects of the crime. Depending on the complexity of the situation, this might mean doing some additional background checks on your own, keeping the individual under careful personal surveillance for a while, seeking the advice of a trusted colleague, consulting a lawyer, or enlisting the help of a professional investigator.

The consequences to you or your company of a bungled confrontation with a suspected spy can range from petty acts of malicious retaliation to costly lawsuits. Even more damaging can be the fact that you may have discovered only one part of a much larger network of espionage—and by making that discovery public, you have alerted the rest of the network to operate even more deviously.

In the event that you decide to personally confront a suspected spy, equip yourself ahead of time with as much documented evidence and supporting data and as many exhibits as you can gather: chronologies, photos, blueprints, time slips, drawings, damaged objects, and so forth. These materials will lend their own impressive weight to your discussion and will spare you the need to verbalize all that you know or suspect.

Rehearse your confrontation ahead of time so that you can formulate intelligent responses to any what-if scenarios. Most important, let the person you confront do most of the talking—in fact, let the person do all the talking he or she wants and then some! The impromptu lies a spy tells when he or she is first approached, *before* you reveal your findings and theories, may be the most telltale evidence of all. Never interrupt suspected spies when they are telling their side of the story. Probe with general, open-ended questions rather than specific questions that can be answered with a "yes" or "no."

If you remain patient and controlled, you will probably give suspected spies enough rope to hang themselves. You certainly should not resort to bullying or entrapment, which can be dangerous procedures for professional spy-catchers, let alone for amateur ones. Of course, the same strategy I have just outlined for handling suspected spies applies equally well to situations involving suspected thieves, who stand a good chance of also being spies.

There is no denying that a do-it-yourself survey can uncover many unpleasant things you'd rather not face, all things being equal. Unfortunately, all things are not equal. Solutions are tidy, but problems aren't. A problem that is left unattended will only grow worse as time goes by. This is especially true in the case of people problems. Aside from the fact that a suspected spy can continue to rip you off, your failure to act in and of itself can result in criminal or corporate liability.

It is also possible that a do-it-yourself survey will *not* provide you with all the information you need to make intelligent assessments, plans, and decisions involving the security of your territory. Such surveys often leave you with a basketful of fuzzy pictures. They show that something is wrong, but they don't specify exactly what it is. Or they reveal that you can be attacked, but not if you have indeed been attacked.

What a do-it-yourself survey always does very well is to tell you more precisely what you *need* to find out if you are to function as productively and safely as possible. You may be able to fill this knowledge gap on your own, with the assistance of others in your organization, or you may decide to draw on the expertise of a professional consultant. The latter course is doubly advisable if the problem involves not just *knowing* what is happening, but also *responding* to what is happening. Under these circumstances, a qualified, objective, and reliable point of view is the best guarantee that you will solve the problem rather than add to it. Let's look now at how experts can help you make a tough job easier.

CHAPTER 7 ?

Those in the Know:

How to Select and Work With Security Consultants

> *"The area of undercover operations raises some unique management problems, but like good lawyers, we don't turn down operations because there is a problem."*
> **William Webster,**
> **Director of the FBI**

Americans abhor a snitch. From our first social encounters in the sandbox through school-age bonding to adult membership in the workforce, we are trained to turn deaf ears and blind eyes to the misdeeds of our associates—as long as those misdeeds do not directly hurt us. "Mind your own business!" is the national credo.

In a corporate enterprise, where it is impossible to draw the line between one employee's "business" and another employee's "business," this national credo causes a major dilemma. Because supervisors, managers, and executives cannot count on their people to report suspicious activities involving co-workers, they are left with only two options: Do their own sleuthing and leave it at that, or do their own sleuthing and hire a professional to continue the job.

By anyone's logic, the most effective and efficient approach is to broaden a personal, necessarily amateur investigation by hiring a professional. Many managers instinctively balk at this idea. "Employers don't much like the idea of spying on their own," admits Frank Pinter, head of the highly successful Acme Commercial Detective Agency in Hollywood, Florida. "Employees are like family. It's like admitting the possibility of your wife cheating. But sometimes an employer *has* to know what is going on!"

There are two kinds of professionals who can help counteract potential or actual business espionage: the security consultant and the undercover investigator. Although many self-described security firms and investigative agencies employ people who perform both functions, and although the functions overlap during specific assignments, it is best to look at them separately for the clearest view of the range of professional help available.

WORKING WITH A SECURITY CONSULTANT

A professional security survey is an expert, comprehensive, and resourceful version of the executive walkthrough described in Chapter 5. Like the security walkthrough, it is an on-site inspection of a house, business, factory, or other facility to assess existing security conditions. The security firm then identifies potential problems and makes cost-effective recommendations to solve them.

The most common (and obvious) indicator that a professional security survey is in order is an unexplained loss of material. Retail inventory shrinkage costs U.S. companies over $2 billion a year, and 70 percent of this shrinkage can be attributed to internal theft or mismanagement. Such losses have a leveraging effect, in that it takes many dollars in increased sales to overcome a single dollar lost. A 7 percent profit margin, for example, requires $214,300 in sales to replace a $15,000 loss!

Other reasons for initiating a professional security survey include getting to the root of safety violations, examining the impact of major changes in the way business is conducted, and checking out irregularities uncovered in a routine security walkthrough. Many managers regularly invest in professional security surveys simply as part of their responsibility to provide a safe and productive work environment.

Once a decision is made to contract a professional security survey, it is wise to think beyond the specific catalyst for that decision to the other possible benefits such a survey could bring.

Here are some answers to questions commonly asked by prospective security agency clients.

What Should I Expect From a Security Consultant?

A professional consultant should be well versed in all aspects of security. Most reliable security firms, mindful of how much a good reputation matters in their industry, conduct extensive management training programs to make sure that their representatives are knowledgeable, diligent, imaginative, trustworthy, and discreet. In researching security companies, it's a good idea to find out how their consultants are trained.

Among other tasks, a security consultant should:

- Help establish survey goals.
- Submit a written proposal covering all the areas you have discussed.
- Provide complete background information on personnel assigned to do the survey.
- Begin gathering relevant data as soon as the proposal is accepted.
- Analyze the data gathered and formulate recommendations.
- Submit regular written reports (including data analysis and recommendations) directly to you and keep them confidential.
- Use computer and specialized skills to your advantage in conducting private research and in presenting information in the form most useful to you.
- Provide follow-up work as needed.

However impeccable a security firm's credentials may be, it cannot operate in a vacuum. Cooperation between the professional security consultant and company security staff is critical. Company personnel should provide the consultant with all security data relevant to the situation; the consultant, in turn, should verify, use, and amplify these data.

Too often, company security people and outside consultants work against each other when they should be working together. One especially memorable incident occurred when I was a management trainee at Pinkerton's Inc.—at that time, the biggest private investigation firm in the country.

I had been an investigator for several years and was doing my first large-scale security survey for a university and research center. The assignment was part of a tough, six-month management training program that featured close supervision and covered both security and investigation procedures. I thought I was ready for anything—and I might have been, if the client hadn't decided to play games. In an effort to test both my firm's expertise and the company's own security measures, the client had deliberately withheld information about how its security systems worked. To make matters worse, my mentor and I were pitted against the existing security team, which was not told about our presence.

My mentor and I began our survey by watching and waiting in a car across the street from one of the hot spots of the institution, the administration building. As the security guard began his rounds, we left the car and followed him at a distance, taking care to keep out of sight. At the foot of a concrete stairwell, the fire door opened easily. At the top of the stairwell, however, the door was locked, and we had not been given the key. When we returned to the first door, we discovered it had locked behind us, and we hadn't been given that key either. We were caught in a classic man-trap and might easily have been discovered by the security guard. Fortunately, my mentor had steel heel clips on his shoes, and I have long arms. We broke the small window in the fire door, reached through, and turned the knob. Later, we called the client, explained what had happened, and paid to replace the window.

The security survey had been needlessly and dangerously complicated. But I did come away from it with an insider's look at a failed operation and a lesson that can benefit both clients and their consultants: Red faces and broken glass make a poor beginning!

How Should I Prepare for Interviewing Security Consultants?

The client must assume control from the start if the survey is to be of maximum use. Before speaking with any security consultant, a company should develop its own written and "sharable" list of what it wants the security survey to accomplish—the results it expects and the steps it feels are necessary to achieve those results.

As the client, you are the expert in your particular area of responsibility. It is up to you to manage problems, rather than cause them. Above all, don't reinvent the wheel. Take what you already know about the facility—floor plans, locking systems, standard security procedures, and informal walkthrough observations—and go from there. If you do, your consultants won't get caught up a stairwell over the weekend; more important, they will do a better job, one with a bottom line that justifies your efforts.

The more specific and detailed your list of security objectives is, the more effective the survey will be. "Risk identification" and "risk reduction" are valid goals, but much too general to be of any practical use in a survey planning session. Good security objectives also specify *why* and *how*.

The steps taken by the operations manager of one international company illustrate how sound objectives are established.

Before calling in any professional help, the manager assembled information about security surveys in general: who does them, what credentials the consultant(s) should have, and what forms the reports should take. He read security magazines and studied relevant data banks. He contacted federal, state, and local law enforcement organizations for free security information pertinent to his industry and geographical area.

During his interviews with prospective security agencies, the manager expressed *his* understanding of a security survey as "a method of collecting information and then translating information into recommendations to reduce both risk and loss at a facility." He then outlined the areas he wanted covered and the appropriate time frames for covering them. He took special care to articulate exactly how he wanted the survey reports prepared: They were to be typed on computer disks formatted for use by IBM-compatible personal computers and typeset so that specific security checklists could be printed out as minimanuals for the various departments within the company. He also stated up front and in writing that he wanted the consultants to gather information and make recommendations as if they "had stock in the company and expected a profit."

To strengthen his point, the manager carefully articulated his business philosophy: "We want someone to come in and walk us through a complete security survey so that we can do smaller surveys ourselves. We use consultants as teachers who work with us on particular projects, not as professors who lecture from afar." He concluded that he expected the survey to yield tangible, "dollars and cents" results from better use of existing security systems and paybacks from new equipment and techniques.

The operations manager then focused on specific security objectives:

- *Physical security* was to be updated to safeguard personnel, the facility itself, and materials and documents stored in the facility. He emphasized, "People come first," and demonstrated this by insisting that all recommended controls be fully explained in commonsense language and easy-to-follow steps.
- *Personnel security* was to include an improved system of background checks so that honest employees were not subjected to dishonest ones.
- *Information security* was to feature much tighter document controls. The manager requested specific plans for reducing the amount and cost of security paperwork. He also requested an assessment of how the company might better use the different modes of processing information: electronic, printed, handwritten, and verbal.

This example highlights three important points:

1. *The results of a security survey must be goal-oriented, with the client setting the goals.* A generic survey, with simple checklists of external lighting, locks, and so on, isn't enough—not if what a company really needs is better control of business secrets or written guidelines for the mail room or the loading dock.
2. *The security consultant must see the client company as a separate and unique entity.* Spend some time explaining your company to the consultant and establishing your management style and philosophy, so that the end result suits both you and your business.
3. *The consultant should know from the outset how the final survey findings are to be presented.* A competitive security firm should be able to format its analyses and recommendations on

computer disks according to a client's specifications. It should also be capable of producing reports that are camera-ready for the printer or targeted to specific audiences (for example, different organizational hierarchies or educational levels).

How Do I Find Good Security Consultants and What Are Their Qualifications?

The American Society for Industrial Security (ASIS) is a good place to start looking for consultants. The society maintains chapters throughout the United States and abroad and runs an excellent testing program that leads to Certified Protection Professional (CPP) status for those who complete it.

Be aware that ASIS members include security equipment salespeople, guard company officials, and others who may find it difficult to be impartial as survey consultants. Check for any possible prejudice or conflict of interest during the initial research interview.

Other good sources for security firm information are the local Better Business Bureau and professional organizations in your industry. It is not wise, however, to ask specific companies in your industry or an allied industry for security firm recommendations, since you may be giving away a vital business secret to a rival. It is also not advisable to seek assistance from a client firm or any other firm with which you routinely do business. The possibility of someone taking unfair advantage of the situation may be slim, but it's not worth the risk.

What Does a Security Survey Cost?

There is no typical or "average" cost for a professional survey. Costs vary widely, depending on the demands of the survey and the qualifications of the consultant. Security companies should have office overhead and staff requirements worked out well in advance, so that they can quote reasonable rates as soon as the client has established a set of survey objectives.

A good survey consultant is a full-time professional, not a part-timer out for a fast buck. When pricing a consultant's services, multiply the hourly rate by forty hours a week and see if the figure sounds reasonable for the education, experience, and expenses of those who will do the work.

How Long Should a Survey Take?

A security survey of a private residence can be done in a day, and the written report of that survey can be submitted within a week. The specific time span, of course, varies according to the size of the residence and the size and nature of the neighborhood. A review of the neighborhood is critical for the survey, since no house or other structure exists in a vacuum.

Most business premises are more extensive than residences and must be surveyed in more detail. Again, average time spans are difficult to project. When an oil exploration company suspected a leak in one of its offices, the office was surveyed within half a day. Later, a complete survey was made of one of the exploration sites—four small one-story buildings, a lab, and a communications trailer. The assignment took three weeks plus another week to write the report.

For most security consultants, time is the slave of function—specifically, the function(s) that the surveyed site fulfills and that the consultant needs to observe. The greater the number of functions involved, the longer the survey will take.

Questor consultants once did a perimeter survey of a warehouse the size of a city block in a day and a night. The warehouse was open only during the day and had good burglar and fire alarms in place, all monitored by in-house security people during the night. If the same warehouse had been in operation around the clock, the consultants would have wanted to observe all three shifts and shift changes and to make an after-hours tour of the neighborhood. The total survey would then have taken close to a week. If the company had also requested a check on internal controls, the survey would have spanned three weeks, plus a week for the written report.

A large manufacturing plant may perform many of the functions of a small town or even a fair-sized city. Most large plants have several different work environments: a cafeteria, a medical office, a library, a gymnasium, and even a chapel—plus a security division that may be larger than a small-town police department. The initial survey of such a plant might take two months, followed by routine surveys performed by the in-house security staff.

WORKING WITH AN UNDERCOVER INVESTIGATOR

Undercover investigation, secret operation, and internal survey are different names for the same thing: planting a detective in a workplace to observe business operations and to report risks, problems, and crimes. Individual agencies and agents choose the terminology that best suits their purpose or fancy. In my view, the term "undercover investigation" most clearly distinguishes this legal and beneficial activity from its sinister shadow: corporate spying.

Legitimate undercover investigators work as regular employees in a client company, not in a rival firm. They are usually on the payroll for at least a month, performing tasks related to their cover job and submitting confidential reports on whatever investigative topics have been established with the client.

A legitimate undercover investigation may catch a thief, clarify deep-seated employee unrest, or spot a hidden bottleneck—results that have a dollar value to the company far greater than the cost of the investigation itself. An honest investigator can provide an honest client with a look at the internal workings of a company that the client cannot get any other way.

Like the professional security survey, the professional undercover investigation is usually occasioned by a large, unaccountable loss of physical materials. Another, less tangible problem that calls for undercover work is a mysterious leak of company information. The information thief is much more difficult to catch than the robber of goods. A skilled professional working undercover, however, has the opportunity not only to identify an employee who is stealing information (either for personal use or for an outsider) but also to collect a solid body of evidence that will support any action a client company may need to take against that employee.

There are countless additional reasons for hiring an undercover agent: waning staff morale, divisive office politics, or inexplicably low productivity; a corporate shake-up (new people, new procedures, new work, or new facilities) that could have significant "front line" effects; repeated examples of suspicious behavior on the part of one employee. Sometimes simple intuition tells a manager that things are not as they should be.

It's one thing to know the benefits of hiring a professional undercover agent or team of agents. It's quite another thing to launch and monitor an actual investigation. Because of their very nature, undercover operations are shrouded in mystery and clouded by misconception. In fact, undercover investigation is much like any other business, and hiring an investigation agency involves the same basic principles as engaging any other business service.

The vast majority of clients who seek out private investigators are honest people who are understandably worried about trafficking in secrets, exposing their companies, or being victimized by incompetent or unscrupulous investigators. Here are some of the issues that are raised most often.

What Should I Do Before Contacting a Private Investigator?

Like the security survey, the undercover investigation calls for a great deal of advance planning. As the client, you should research the subject in general and your own needs in particular. Set investigation goals and activities that are as specific and as detailed as possible. Develop a clear picture of your company's unique character and your particular business philosophy, one that you can communicate to potential investigators. Itemize all your expectations and requirements, especially in regard to the content and format of investigative reports.

What Is an Undercover Agent Like?

The typical legitimate undercover agent is a fairly recent college graduate with postgraduate investigative and/or security training. The relative youth of such agents enables them to blend more easily into a typical work environment. Of course, an atypical workplace (for example, a senior citizens' residence or a nurses' quarters) may call for an atypical agent. The agents' training helps ensure that they possess the talent, intelligence, stamina, and moral commitment to warrant the trust of employers and clients.

The best operative is the one who best fits a particular assignment. In the investigative field it is survival of the fittest—not the biggest or the toughest, necessarily, but the agent who fits!

Here is an example of how critical the issue of fitness can be. The manager of a warehouse that employed a large number of Mexican immigrants contracted a Spanish-speaking American of Mexican descent to conduct an undercover investigation, posing as a regular employee. There was only one handicap the agent would have to overcome to succeed in his impersonation: a solidly middle class background that set him apart from the other workers.

On his first day of work, the agent was careful to bring his lunch in a plain paper bag. When lunchtime rolled around and all the workers gathered together, the agent knew he was being carefully scrutinized. He pulled his lunch out of his bag—a steak sandwich. The other workers pulled their lunches out of their bags—tortillas and beans. The agent's game was over, and he did not report to work the next day.

What this story suggests is that the successful undercover agent is someone who not only looks the part but also can think far and fast. According to Kevin Peterson, president of Intelligence Services, a New York City firm with about fifty investigators-for-hire, "Undercover agents have to be people who thrive on tension, they have to be good actors, and they have to be clever."

Successful undercover agents also tend to know, and like, a wide variety of people. It is no coincidence that many of them have had sales training or public service experience. Many private investigators are former government agents. I once was lucky enough to have a former Scotland Yard inspector, a former deputy U.S. marshal, and several former U.S. military intelligence officers on my staff at the same time. Our personnel man came from the CIA. Not many agencies are so fortunate.

How Does a Typical Undercover Investigation Work?

No undercover investigation is routine. Still, it is possible to develop a representative scenario of how an investigation is initiated and what steps an investigator usually takes. When a manager calls a private investigative agency, the agency usually assigns a supervisor to the case—a person who may or may not end up being the actual undercover agent during the investigation. The supervisor then meets with the prospective client, away from the company, to discuss investigative goals and procedures. If the client decides to give the agency a contract for an undercover operation, the billing goes to the client's home and all payments are made to the agency under the accountant's name.

At this point, an agent is assigned. With the help of the client and the agency, the investigator develops a checklist of possible subjects for future reports. These subjects include:

- First impressions of the client company and its hiring procedures (which the agent, of course, will experience firsthand).

- The client's special problems—loss of inventory, property damage, sabotage, procedural bottlenecks, organizational conflicts.

- Employee attitudes toward corporate objectives and policies, management structure and personnel, pay and benefits, and working conditions.

- Unusual or injurious employee activities, such as agitation, slowdowns in productivity, drug usage, and sexual harassment.

- The nature, extent, and appropriateness of employee supervision.

- The effectiveness of corporate security.

- Fire and safety hazards.

- Potential trouble spots in the espionage war—unguarded loading docks, free-access computer rooms, poorly situated lounge areas, unauthorized exits, places where spies can hide or contraband can be concealed.

This assignment-related list (which is memorized rather than carried as a document), is accompanied by a set of tacit general instructions:

1. *Submit a written report at the end of each working day.* Report only what you see and hear. Don't tell clients how to run their businesses—tell them how their businesses are being run!

2. *Compose reports in the third person so that you are less likely to be exposed if the report gets into the wrong hands.* For example, if you, Barbara Smith, have a conversation with John Doe, write: "John Doe and Barbara Smith were overheard discussing. . . ."

3. *Don't name the client company in reports.*

4. *Use the assigned code number and mail all reports to the agency post office box.* Use the exact postage. Do not give a return address.

5. *Discuss several topics in each report.* Concentrate on the client's special problems, but cover every item on the checklist at some time during the investigation.

6. *Be specific, accurate, and thorough about "who, what, where, and when."*

7. *After-hours expenses incurred with other company employees are justified if your report shows results.* Pay particular attention to co-workers who seem to have a source of income other than their salaries.

8. *Be positive when possible.* An exceptionally good employee should be pointed out as readily as an exceptionally bad one.

9. *If you must call the agency supervisor while on an undercover assignment, don't use a phone that goes through an in-house switchboard or switching system.* Maintain confidentiality.

10. *Be cautious with any materials that could identify your role as an agent (e.g., your real name), the agency, or the specific client.* Don't leave these materials where others can see them.

11. *Put the client's interests first.* As you go about your daily work, ask yourself: "How might this situation affect the client's business?" Every single observation or contact you make can provide an insight into how the business is actually being run— or stopped—behind the scenes. This is true whether you're working undercover as an executive assistant to the chairman or as a parts runner in a shop.

What Does Undercover Work Cost?

As of this writing, the agency fee for undercover work begins at about $20 per hour, though it varies considerably in different parts of the country and from agency to agency. In addition, a client usually pays an agreed-upon base salary for the agent's cover job. Agents, therefore, have two incomes—and employers. What they make as "regular" company employees they keep, plus they are paid by the investigative agency for compiling their daily reports.

How Long Does It Take to Start Getting Results?

An undercover agent usually needs a week or two to become familiar with a company and to gain the confidence of other employees to the point where they will begin to talk about irregularities or problems. Meanwhile, the agent can report on how he or she was processed into the company, safety violations, and other easily observable items on the assignment-related checklist. During a well-conducted operation, a report covering two or more subjects of interest to the client should be submitted every day, beginning with the first day.

What Happens When the Agent Catches a Thief or Spots a Serious Problem?

Investigators are not snitches. They are the client's eyes and ears inside the company. They take *no* overt action that would expose themselves, their agencies, or their clients. An undercover investigator may see a co-worker leaving the premises loaded down with stolen merchandise. The agent may hold the door open, help the other employee into a car, and soon become an insider with a group that has been stealing from the company for years. The information will be turned over to agency investigators outside the company, so that the undercover agent can remain in place to make sure everyone involved is identified.

In a more urgent situation, the undercover agent may have to call the agency supervisor (from an outside line) and ask for immediate assistance so that the operation is not exposed. In extreme situations involving an immediate safety hazard or physical threat, the undercover agent will do what any responsible employee on the job would do to comply with company policy and basic principles of human decency.

What Are the Chances That an Undercover Operative Will Be Exposed?

It is highly unlikely that a competent agent will be exposed by co-workers since the agent deliberately avoids any overt espionage activity on the job. This course of behavior has a strong, built-in motivation. It protects the agent and the agency, as well as the client. On those rare occasions when agents are exposed (or when agents suspect possible exposure), they quickly withdraw from the workplace, leaving co-workers in the dark about the motives behind or the beneficiaries of their activities.

FINDING THE RIGHT PROFESSIONAL FOR YOUR NEEDS

As useful as this discussion of security consultants and undercover agents may be, it is an overview only. Individual consulting firms and investigative agencies differ greatly in the quality and variety of services that their personnel provide. Some examples:

- A small private detective agency in California has only one good investigator in the office—the owner. His presentation to new clients is impressive, but the performance of his underpaid and poorly trained field agents is not.
- A larger, Midwestern agency is all legwork. The office computers are used solely as word processors to turn out generic reports that look like originals. No one on the staff can access the business data banks or perform any of the countless other functions that computers can do to assist a security survey or undercover investigation. What most attracts clients to this firm is its good camera work.
- An East Coast outfit at the other end of the scale does virtually nothing but computer work. Staff members seldom leave the office, even to verify questionable data. They merely download off the data banks onto their own disks, rework the information so

that it looks like an investigative report, and hit the PRINT key on the keyboard.

The issue here is not that individual companies may misrepresent themselves or be deficient in some critical way. More important, individual companies may deliberately restrict themselves to certain areas of proficiency in order to maintain a competitive edge. The security and investigation industry is growing and changing rapidly. In the very near future, countermeasures managers may have to deal with firms so specialized that it will be difficult to evaluate their overall capabilities. One firm may do private computer research, another may do employee background checks, a third may specialize in field operations. The countermeasures manager may want to call upon all three, on separate assignments or in combination, depending on the company's needs.

Four guidelines can help client companies cope with this potentially bewildering diversity:

1. *Know your operative.* The agency may not want you to meet face to face with the investigator for security reasons, but it is not unreasonable to expect the agency to give you background information. You may want to know the investigator's educational experience, how long he or she has been with the agency, and whether the agent has worked your type of case before. You may want to see a copy of the investigator's résumé, even if specific names and addresses must be blanked out.

Remember that the agency representative at the interview may not be doing the actual work. Make sure that the operative in your survey or undercover investigation is fully qualified to perform all the tasks that the assignment requires.

2. *Have a clear understanding of what work is to be done and what you will be getting in the final report.* "No problem" or "nothing happened" is not acceptable. "No new information was developed" does not justify the fees. A client has the right to know what avenues the consultant or investigator explored—and how—so that it does not go over the same ground.

If the operative dug through old records in the basement of the courthouse, the report should say so and specify which records were checked, even if nothing of apparent value turned up. If a computer run of *Standard & Poor's Corporate Descriptions* fails to turn up anything of value from the more than 7,800 U.S. companies listed, this should be spelled out in the report. *D&B—Principal International Businesses* may be the next place to look. Clients need specific details. "We ran the data banks with negative results" is just not good enough.

3. *Insist on absolute confidentiality.* Most client companies assume that what they tell a security consultant or undercover agent about their business and what the consultant or agent discovers on assignment are both strictly confidential. This is not always the case.

A security agency once photocopied a partially blacked-out report as a sample to be used by its sales staff in soliciting new clients. Unfortunately, only one large company in that field did business along the lines shown in the report. Many people who saw the "carefully edited" text could easily fill in the blanks. The agency defended its action by saying, "The client didn't say we couldn't use the report."

4. *Be sure the agency's physical security is at least as good as your own.* The old adage that shoemakers' children have no shoes applies to several companies in various parts of the United States.

One agency keeps client reports in old-fashioned metal filing cabinets with nothing more than the flimsy original built-in locks between any outsider and vital business secrets. More than one of its client firms use bar locks on filing cabinets as part of a comprehensive security program. They probably think their investigative agency does too.

The same agency is on the ground floor of a building with burglar alarm switches on the windows and doors, but no interior space alarms. There is an electrical outlet on the outside of the building for use by the gardeners, and the building has unsecured crawlspace in the basement and wood floors. A burglar or spy with an electric chain saw has it made!

In short, check out professional investigators before they check out you. Naturally, a client can't conduct as thorough a survey or investigation as a competent professional agency can. But a reasonable inquiry into the qualifications of the company and its agents, coupled with a reasonable degree of control over how the work is conducted, will do much to safeguard the undercover operation.

CHAPTER 8

Being Computer Conscious:

How to Safeguard Your Information Systems

> *"The greatest influence for good or evil is not man at all. It is a machine: the computer."*
> **Time, touting the computer as Man of the Year (1982)**

Over the past thirty years, the computer has revolutionized our world, greatly enhancing the range of possibilities affecting how we conduct our businesses, how we live our daily lives, and even how we think. Unfortunately, the computer has also revolutionized the subworld of espionage, fraud, sabotage, and thievery.

Because computer intelligence is so vulnerable to invasion and manipulation, electronic vandals are far more powerful and difficult to trap than their clumsy, precomputer counterparts. Even at remote distances, they can easily gain access to trade secrets; effect transfers of funds, documents, and merchandise; and alter records as they see fit—for profit, for vengeance, or for the sheer thrill of it all.

Thomas Whiteside, author of *Computer Capers: Tales of Electronic Embezzlement and Fraud* (New York: Thomas Y. Crowell, 1978), points out that the intellectual challenge offered by computer invasion is rapidly attracting a whole new breed of formidable crooks. "It's a form of breaking and entering," Whiteside explains, "in which the burglar's tools are essentially an understanding of the logical structure of, and logical flaws inherent in, particular programming and processing systems."

Aiding and abetting the computer criminal is the phenomenal rate of change in computer technology. So far, security mechanisms—and security countermeasures—have failed to keep pace. Inadequate protection of computer intelligence is a problem at each and every level, from supersecret government agencies to mobile coffee vendors who must guard the information stored on their pushcart PCs. These statistics illustrate just how serious the problem is:

■ Keith Davidson, executive director of XPLOR, an association of users and managers of electronic printing systems, maintains that 90 percent of corporate documents are now captured electronically. This means that the scope of material available to a would-be destroyer or misuser is almost total.

■ A single incident of computer crime can result in extensive damage. A survey conducted by the National Center for Crime Data and reported in *Security World* (February 1986) cited the average physical harm to computer data or programs at $93,600 per incident and the average loss due to theft of information at $81,000 per incident.

■ The American Bar Association reported computer-related thefts involving 136 public and private American companies in 1986, with total damages running between $145 million and $730 million (depending on long-range consequences).

■ Many single criminal acts result in multimillion-dollar losses. Current estimates of nationwide losses begin at a staggering $1 billion a year, according to *Lotus* magazine (Steve Stecklow, "Computer Crime Is on the Rise," September 1986). The figure may be much higher, since most computer crimes are unreported. Add to this the chilling fact that a countless number of computer crimes go undetected!

The worst is yet to come, as the Information Age continues to produce information junkies. For the time being, there is no computer system in existence that can't be penetrated. In the words of Dana Parker, a computer expert who advises the Pentagon, "The perfectly secure computer is one you can't use."

PROFILE OF A HACKER

The most likely culprit in a corporate computer crime is a programmer or other technician within the company itself. But the model for such a criminal is the amateur hacker—the outsider who possesses a personal computer, a modem, and the morals of a joyrider.

The typical neighborhood prowler has no "grand scheme." He steals through night shadows trying one house or garage door after another, then trying cars at the curb. No attempt is made to break in and no sophisticated burglary tools are used—no "burning bar," no hydraulic splitters. The prowler simply tries the doors to see if anyone has been foolish enough to leave them open.

This is the way most computer hackers work. They try electronic doors to see what has been left unlocked, to see who is using simple access codes instead of more sophisticated call-back techniques. With a certain type of smart modem (signal modulator/demodulator) the thrill-seeking hacker has the potential to do any and all of the following:

- Make and answer computer calls over ordinary telephone lines.

- Send and receive computer files.

- Set up data sessions with unattended remote computer systems.

- Manage communications parameters.

- Facilitate error-free transfers of remote access files.

- Store batch commands for automatic remote communications at specified times.

- Emulate (imitate) other terminals.

- Sort directory entries automatically.

- Switch between voice and data communications at will.

"Most hackers are relatively benign," comments David R. Wilson, national director of Ernst & Whinney, a consulting group that advises business clients in both technical and organizational approaches to computer security. "For hackers, breaking into computers is sport and access to data is merely the scorecard. The greatest threat from hackers is that they provide a roadmap for knowledgeable outsiders to break into a system."

Often this roadmap takes the form of an electronic bulletin board, where hackers proudly display the nitty-gritty details of their accomplishments. As a rule, hacker bulletin boards have better security than many large computer systems—certainly better than the systems hackers have been able to penetrate. To get on a hacker bulletin board, applicants have to give their name, telephone number, place of employment, and information on their driver's license. They may also need a recommendation from a hacker already on the board and/or a signed statement that they are not connected with law enforcement and won't reveal what they learn.

Access to a hacker bulletin board opens up a world of passwords, identification codes, and computer phone numbers that can penetrate a variety of computer systems. For example, one bulletin board spelled out step-by-step instructions for getting inside a key computer system operated by Pacific Telephone and Telegraph Co. in Los Angeles. A recent issue of *Tap,* an underground computer newsletter based in New York, gave the telephone number and other crucial entry details for breaking into the computer of a major university.

The mere knowledge that hackers can and do break into computer systems encourages others to try, especially those who have enough understanding of the organization behind the system to exploit any data they acquire. Companies that discover a hacker in their midst have cause to feel alarmed. If a hacker can penetrate the company's computer system, so can a competitor or an insider.

HIGH-RISK COMPUTER SYSTEMS

The biggest danger in computer theft is ignorance. "People don't realize the extent to which their systems are being broken into," says Clifton M. Garrott, Los Angeles deputy district attorney for electronic crimes. Here's a look at some of the ways computers are used in legitimate businesses and the various risks involved.

Computers in Research and Development

Computers play a major role in basic laboratory research and in product and service development beyond the lab. Almost all R&D paperwork is processed electronically, from the first experimental data to the final order forms. Every stage of the process is in jeopardy. Summary R&D proposals may be very attractive to another research firm. Details of fabrication processes may be of interest to a rival manufacturer. A service organization may go after consultants' reports.

New computer systems are installed with simple passwords like DEMO, SYSTEM, and TEST. Low-profile ivory-tower R&D groups rarely change these start-up codes. When they do, they usually choose acronyms that are dangerously easy to guess. This was the situation during the "hacker scare" of the late 1970s, when a young, unemployed hacker named Burt Sloane shook up R&D firms across the nation by cracking the codes for the MIT Artificial Intelligence Lab Computer, thereby gaining access to the entire system.

The prime targets of hackers are user-friendly systems like those in most R&D departments and other areas where large numbers of people with varying degrees of computer literacy need to have access to the same data. These systems should *not* be difficult to use, but even a basic precaution such as leaving the vowels out of passwords can make them far more hacker-proof. An espionage file, for example, can be coded SPNG, a password much harder to guess than ESP or SPI.

Hardened computer systems are particularly advisable for research and development groups. Such systems might include electronic scramblers, dedicated lines, and audit trails. Also important is careful control of who is in the area when critical material is being processed. Many systems break down in the absence of this last precaution.

A financial services representative making sales calls on new companies was taken on a tour of a high-tech biochemicals firm. He watched lab assistants input data and even saw one of them punch in the start-up code for a customized software program designed to monitor research equipment. Since the sales call had nothing to do with R&D, the sales rep should have been kept away from the computer area.

Computers in Market Research

Demographic information is the lifeblood of market research, and it attracts all sorts of vampires, from direct business competitors to individual entrepreneurs intent on launching their own "mom and pop" operation with the help of a stolen data base. What makes this type of information especially vulnerable is the fact that it is often compiled on disks that are laughably easy to access.

Many government agencies now provide vital demographic data to the business world on computer disks. The four most significant agencies are the Bureau of Labor Statistics, the Bureau of Economic Analysis, the Bureau of the Census, and the National Technical Information Service. The widespread availability and use of this information alarms databank librarians, who are accustomed to having such data under their judicious control. What interests corporate spies, however, is not the information on the government disks (which they can often get directly from the source), but the disks themselves—*after they have been reworked by a company to serve its particular needs*. A surprising number of marketing teams use the original government disk, or a backup copy, as the foundation for their own statistical library!

The heavy volume of favors and interpersonal exchanges among market research people only aggravates the situation. Many computer users still do not realize that various "ungoof" software programs can read disks that have supposedly been erased. One marketing executive borrowed a statistical information disk on an informal "shareware" basis from another company. The disk still contained two files from the previous owner. He called the owner of the disk and warned him that the DELETE A FILE command on his company's software program had evidently removed the two files from the menu but left them on the disk itself, available to anyone until they were written over. The files in question were labeled MARKET.PRG and CPA.NTS. It doesn't take a computer hacker to guess the subjects of the files!

Computers in Sales

The sales rep armed with a portable computer is a combination whose time has come. Any phone booth can now be a computer message center and order desk. So can the cellular "phone booth" in the sales rep's car.

Small computers are extremely vulnerable out in the field. They are often used in areas that are less secure than company premises and over telephone lines that have fewer controls. For a knowledgeable spy who has the sales rep under surveillance and uses portable electronic bugs, the PC-in-the-field is a wide-open target.

A few weeks ago I saw a man using a laptop computer to prepare sales reports while enjoying the noontime sun in Pike Place Market, a popular outdoor gathering place near the Seattle business district. When I stopped to talk with him, he told me he was just out of college and was working as a pharmaceuticals sales rep on "hospital hill," which overlooks the downtown area. Like many young businesspeople, he grew up with computers and was comfortable with them to the point where he could say, "I don't give them a second thought." This attitude can be dangerous!

As I discussed computers with him, it became apparent that business espionage controls and countermeasures had not been a part of the entry-level orientation program at his company. I showed him a 6 × 15 monocular that is exactly 2 inches long and 1.75 inches wide. It fits easily in the palm of the hand and is popular with "spooks" who do surveillance work in crowds or anywhere else that full-size binoculars would be conspicuous. "I come to the market at least twice a week, have lunch, and work on my reports," the sales rep admitted. "Anyone could read over my shoulder from here or from up the hill!"

He added that he always parked in the same lot on Western Avenue below Pike Place Market and kept his route books and a large batch of 3.5-inch floppy disks in his car, chock-full of such information as sales figures, profit margins, long-range sales plans, production and distribution problems within the company, supplier and supply rosters, and customer profiles. Car prowlers are common in any large public area where people go to relax. If the sales rep's car were broken into by business spies, he would probably write it off as a routine burglary by one of the local muscatel-for-lunch bunch who panhandle from tourists and sleep under the viaduct. I hope our talk made him a little more savvy.

Computers in Training

Tutorials, video disks, interactive software, and other informational and instructional media run by computer can help train or retrain employees at their own speed and without supervision. This cuts training costs. It also enables trainees to make private copies of important company materials without being observed. Many training programs feature detailed descriptions of technical matters or production processes that would be very valuable to competitors. I once handled a case involving the illegal sale of a training tape that demonstrated how a soft drink is frothed to produce its distinctively creamy head.

An associate of mine, a former teacher who specializes in training materials, received a call from a well-known training expert in another organization. The caller asked for a copy of a computerized training program—to be used, in her words, "only as an outline for a program I am writing." My associate turned her down, and the caller replied, "Well, that's okay. I know somewhere else I can get it." She promptly called another contact and asked to review the program on her computer monitor by modem. While reviewing the program over the phone, she downloaded the information onto a blank computer disk. Her second contact in this instance was either too lenient or too ignorant to protect the information.

Computers in Customer Service

For customer service reps, tracking orders and shipments by computer has several advantages. Speed and accountability are only two of the more obvious. Allowing customers themselves to tap into the system to track their orders makes for good customer relations and is becoming an increasingly common practice. Unfortunately, spies for the competition can pose as customers and take advantage of this practice.

An acquaintance of mine in the courier business rarely hesitates to let customers use his computers, since customer service is one of the few real "points of difference" in his field. He's convinced that competitors regularly check out his company's procedures and effectiveness by running a pretext package through his system—he's convinced, no doubt, because he does the same thing to his competitors. Because of his lax controls, customers can examine a screen full of information when a single line display is all they need and all they normally should be offered. By tracking small orders through a system at different locations and in different ways, agents often gather considerable information about the inner workings of a company at little cost or risk to themselves.

Computerized mailing-label codes pose another high risk. Because computerized mailing lists can handle customer information so efficiently (it is possible to list twenty-five items or more for each customer), companies are tempted to overload them with data. Regrettably, some customer codes that wind up on shipping labels may reveal more than a company intends about its customers and its methods of serving them.

Because my associates and I at Questor carefully follow trends in electronic equipment, we are on a lot of mailing lists. We always study the codes on the computerized mailing labels as they come in. Not long ago we were amused to see DNRAFO on one of these codes. DNRAFO means "Does not respond after first offer." We now know it is time to follow up on requests!

Computers in Financial Management

Computer links between companies and banks usually mean that better financial information will be available more quickly when decisions must be made. Other financial information may be going in house and out through local area networks (LANs). Spies may attempt to tap into primary sources leading to and from the bank or to break into computer networks within the company itself. Inside lines may be especially vulnerable since businesspeople often think of in-house transactions as "just talking to ourselves."

Jana Pobiarzyn of The Questor Group specializes in personal computer accounting systems and has talked with a great variety of organizations—from credit unions, investment firms, and technical institutes to forest products corporations, food store chains, and fisheries. In installing their first PCs or expanding existing systems, almost all of these companies encountered serious espionage risks because:

1. They failed to include business espionage controls and countermeasures as part of their planning during the changeover to small, decentralized computer systems.
2. They "farmed out" all or part of the work of transferring existing company records into the computer, or they hired new people to do this—people about whom they knew very little.
3. They laid out all the facts and figures on the innermost workings of their company at a time when those records were being subjected to financial software manipulation (what-if accounting and financial planning scenarios) for the first time.

Careful security planning is essential during any changeover involving computerized technology—especially accounting systems that depend on personal computers. Such planning should feature consideration of espionage controls and countermeasures right from the start, staffing a responsible and trustworthy crew to implement the changeover, and strategic timing of the different activities directly and indirectly affecting the changeover.

Selling Computer Time

Many companies think of off-peak computer time as just another surplus product: It is simply something to be sold at the best possible price. They may market existing computer services to outsiders or develop a new service specifically for this purpose. When a company sells surplus computers, it can see buyers out the door and lock up behind them. When a company sells computer time, it keeps its door wide open and leaves buyers to their own devices!

If employees directly connected with selling computer time are not carefully briefed on security matters, they will almost certainly give away company secrets with their sales pitch. If their "customer" is a business spy who is adept at subtle questioning, the odds against the company are unbeatable.

One investigation agency tested this premise quite openly by calling several companies that offer surplus in-house computer time in the form of services to the general public. One such incident involved a new computer typesetting service offered by a multifaceted firm well established in several other fields. Any outside company with a computer and modem could use the service by sending copy to be typeset over the telephone lines.

The manager of the typesetting operation was a computer expert, but not a controls and countermeasures expert. The investigating agent was just a voice on the phone, but the seller talked computers until the agent knew a great deal more than she needed—or asked—to know. The manager discussed his company, his equipment, and how he used it in daily operations within his firm. He even offered to loan the agent a small computer and modem to get her started using the service. A spy with more sophisticated equipment might well have broken past the simple barriers and accessed the entire company network!

The phone-in typesetting service had several weaknesses. The computer access codes were easy to use and easy to guess. There was no call-back procedure to verify the source of a call before processing commands. As for the unwitting customer, anything sent in to be typeset (for example, technical training manuals, executive reports, business plans, or market research data) was accessible to any computer-literate pirate using the service!

A basic call-back procedure to verify customers won't entirely eliminate these security risks, but it will greatly reduce them. Aside from this precaution, the best defense is ongoing awareness of a computer's vulnerability. Computer time-share customers must, of course, be told in detail what a service can do for them, but they should not be told what the service can do for itself.

THE FOUR TYPES OF COMPUTER CRIME

The Federal Deposit Insurance Corporation (FDIC) has established four different types of computer crime:

1. *Physical:* tangible damage to the system's hardware or software, violation of access controls, and theft of computer-related materials.

2. *Transactional:* unauthorized use of a computer system.
3. *Programming:* unauthorized altering of a computer system's transactional functions.
4. *Electronic:* bugging a computer system.

It may be impossible to gain complete control over all four FDIC categories of computer crime, but there are basic guidelines on how to minimize the risks associated with each type of crime.

Physical Crimes

Physical security for computer systems is usually concerned with (1) fire prevention, (2) access controls, and (3) special problems associated with a particular business.

1. *Fire prevention is vitally important to managers concerned about business espionage controls and countermeasures.* Spies often cover their presence by staging fires to divert attention or destroy evidence. They may also set fires to postpone a spy hunt. Finally, a fire is often an act of sabotage by a competitor or a disgruntled employee—someone who is capable of striking countless other times against the company.

2. *Access controls keep out spies as well as thieves, not to mention spies who present themselves as thieves to mask their real objectives.* A man who claimed to be a former insurance investigator now in private practice once walked into Questor's offices. He said he wanted to work with Questor to expose a client who had asked him to spy on someone else. His story was so complicated that it took some time to check it out. When the dust settled, his "client" turned out to be a former employer who had fired him for stealing from the company. The man had harbored two ambitions: to get revenge by setting up his former employer as a master spy and to trick Questor into paying him for bogus information!

3. *Every business has special physical security problems associated with site, climate, and so many other variables that most "generic" and "checklist" computer security surveys barely scratch the surface.* One survey of a research laboratory located in a downtown office building revealed an unusual source of property loss. The researchers there were doing a long-term study and kept hundreds of what appeared to be the oldest mice in the world on the premises. Over time, the researchers had come to regard these mice as pets, and the mice were allowed to wander freely across desk tops while they were being weighed, measured, and tested. Some of the mice had disappeared inside personal computers: The disk drive openings were just mouse-sized and perhaps the units retained enough heat to attract old bones!

Beyond fire hazards, access violations, and special company-related problems looms the ever present danger of outright theft. The item most at risk in computer crime turns out to be the computer itself, especially the personal computer. The information a computer processes may be more valuable, but the computer hardware is often easier to steal, as this case history suggests.

Case History 7: Actual Inc.

The PCs at Actual Inc. were fastened down with cable that could be cut with ordinary pliers. Bolts or tempered chain are much better, and locking covers are better yet, since they not only prevent the computers from being removed but also render them inoperable after hours.

Many of the operators at Actual Inc. tucked "cheat sheets" of commands and other codes under their PCs. Given the relative sophistication of most PC crimes, it's safe to assume that thieves will take these sheets along with the computer. They may, in fact, be more interested in the sheets than the computer, but they will still take both to make the crime look like a routine theft.

The mainframe computer at Actual Inc. was just off a hallway leading to a poorly lit parking lot. The double doors to the outside were secured by a lock in the middle that shot a 1-inch dead bolt door to door. This might have been a strong defense, except that there were ¼-inch gaps near the hinges and between the two doors: enough room for a tire iron to work its way in and pop the dead bolt out of its socket!

The computer room had a more secure entrance, featuring single metal doors with tight dead-bolt locks. Unfortunately, however, the locks on the doors were the same make as the ones on the outside doors and could be opened by the same master key. A separate system is far more secure. Even more effective is a card key lock.

Apparently the people who designed the computer center at Actual Inc. had not looked at building blueprints carefully and asked themselves: "What is inside or just beyond the walls of the computer center? What is above the ceiling? What is below the floor?" There were unsecured crawlspaces immediately adjacent to the center where thieves and spies could hide. Spies could also run wires and plant wireless equipment in these crawlspaces or take similar advantage of the unsecured openings around plumbing and air-conditioning units shared by the computer center and an upstairs coffee lounge.

The most serious weakness I've described—that the computer room locks could be opened by the same master key as the outside door locks—was at one time exploited by the sales manager. He entered the computer room after hours and ran copies of customer lists and other data that he took with him when he left to start his own firm.

Actual Inc. was forced into litigation against this new competitor, but the damage had already been done.

Computer security extends not just to the computer center itself but to the tape and disk library, the programmers' offices, the computer maintenance and repair areas, the supply rooms that serve computer activities, and the office of the manager directly responsible for computer operations. Here are some points to keep in mind:

1. Adequate perimeter lighting, locks, and alarms are essential to stop thieves and spies in *any* area of a business plant.

2. The tape and disk library should be housed in a secured area that is outside the computer room and not directly accessible to it. Data control is almost impossible if computer tapes and disks are kept in the same room as the computer. Individual tapes and disks should be checked out as needed and should always be accounted for.

3. Programmers' offices should be set off from the main computer room but have the same level of security.

4. For efficiency's sake, the computer maintenance and repair room needs to open directly into the main computer area. It should have a separate door and lock, however.

5. The computer center should have its own supply room so that traffic through the center can be better monitored and controlled. Because of the fire hazard posed by large quantities of flammable paper goods, the supply room should be close to but separate from the computer room as well as from the tape and disk library.

6. The manager's office needs especially tight security. It is the hub of the computer center, and it can also be where all the aspects of company operations come together! Anything requiring masses of data that only a computer can organize effectively—such as procedural manuals, statistical analyses, and long-range planning reports—may be found in this one office, in the form of raw notes, in-progress printouts, or final hard copy.

The computer manager's office should have a separate zone on the alarm system and separate entrance controls. We often recommend entrance controls that require the use of personal codes and that automatically record the time and date.

One computer center manager had developed the habit of stacking information for the next day's processing in a red file folder. The manager would then proceed to lock that folder overnight in an ordinary metal desk. What office prowler does not know how to open a metal desk with a pair of long-nose vise-grip pliers? The manager would be well advised not to print out any information until shortly before it's needed and, once it is printed, to keep it in a safe.

Transactional Crimes

One of the biggest threats to any computer system is unauthorized access to workstations, whereby knowledgeable insiders or outsiders can enter the system and perform transactions that will benefit them and/or hurt the company. In recent years this threat has increased immeasurably with the proliferation of desktop PCs in unsecured areas that are linked to one another, to the mainframe computer, and to LANs.

Most people associate physically large computers with the handling of major transactions. With today's sophisticated technology, however, big more properly refers to capacity rather than bulk size. In most business environments, the risk of computer espionage does not decrease in proportion to the smallness of the computer. In many companies, the opposite is true!

One office services company used an expensive backup computer with two 30Mb hard-disk drives. Often referred to as a 30/30 (or Winchester, for obvious reasons), the computer was locked away in a room by itself. As time went on and computers got smaller, the company purchased a Winchester hard-disk drive for a desktop PC that gave the PC virtually the same capacity as the 30/30. Because the PC was so much less expensive and less intimidating than the 30/30, managers decided to leave it in an open office so that more people could use it. Thinking only in terms of price and appearance, they overlooked the risks posed by the computer's power. Financial and other information once restricted to top management and the inner circle of the computer center was suddenly available—actually or potentially—to anyone with the will to take it!

There is no ideal controls and countermeasures system for preventing transactional computer crimes. But one thing is certain: The most effective system combines both hardware and software features. Such a system may have a plug-in board and supporting software to control all aspects of computer operation. It probably includes an encryption (or encoding) component and two or more codes. It most certainly produces an audit trail and an alert when attempts are made to defeat the system's security mechanisms.

Programming Crimes

Unscrupulous, angry, or desperate people who know more about a computer system than just its access codes or physical safeguards can steal information or divert funds by altering the computer programs themselves. They need not possess the title of programmer: Many computer buffs know one or more computer languages and are capable of complicated programming maneuvers.

Most people who commit programming crimes are authorized users of the system—users intent on subverting the system to their own ends. Typically, they create fraudulent records to cover the transfer of funds to themselves or a third party, or else they program a "standing order" or "duplicate order" into a data system so that each time information is added they get a copy.

A sales executive for one typesetting firm was an amateur expert in computing. He and several other executives with the company had access to the mainframe computer and used it to play sophisticated computer games and to perform other routines unrelated to business. Not all the games were innocent. The sales executive had built his own private source of top-level leads by adding a "modifier" to the company's database program that flagged new entries and printed them for him at his command.

It is not uncommon for programmers to use "programming time" or "engineering time" for their own purposes. They may only play computer games or contact friends via the communications protocol. Still, the seductive urge to experiment may eventually produce an in-house hacker. Think of computer time as part of inventory; then think of inventory controls!

Electronic Crimes

Business espionage agents often attach electronic bugs directly to one or more of the cables that link the different components of the computer system. In local area networks, a spy may use compatible equipment to become part of the "network bus," the "network star," or the "network ring." All cable links should be checked both visually and electronically on a regular basis, but not necessarily at regular times.

Spies can even plant electronic bugs to catch signals from unsecured or unshielded computer equipment without touching the target system itself. Electronic pulses passing through wire produce force fields that are capable of being read by sensors placed near the wire. This type of bug is difficult to spot since it is not actually connected to the wiring and may look like a piece of molding or other familiar object. Electronic debugging procedures are examined in Chapter 9.

FIGHTING COMPUTER CRIME: SEVEN STEPS

Controls and countermeasures begin with people. The best physical and electronic safeguards are only as good as the operators who use them. At their best, these controls are still far from foolproof against a determined criminal. Here are seven major steps for waging war against computer crime.

1. *Check the credentials of everyone who has access to the computer system.* Screen candidates closely for any full-time, part-time, or project-term computer work. Train key computer operators in basic counterespionage techniques for the particular types of software used by the system.

2. *Take an active role in setting antiespionage priorities, establishing appropriate controls and countermeasures, and testing those controls and countermeasures frequently to make sure of their effectiveness.* Many highly competent security professionals are so busy with routine security matters that they do not have time for dealing with all the subtleties involved in preventing computer espionage. They may also lack the management background to properly assess computer espionage risks. The ideal control is a counterespionage team made up of selected security people and managers from different departments.

3. *Develop a "disaster plan" if one does not already exist.* Begin by making sure that all company contingency plans take the computer system into account. Ask yourself: "What happens in the event of a fire or a bomb scare or vandalism? Is there backup power to run the computers? Are backup data secure at another site?"

4. *Investigate access controls at regular intervals, but not on a fixed schedule that can be predicted by a clever thief or spy.* The investigation should cover perimeter controls, computer hardware controls, and software control systems. All members of the management team should take part in these investigations.

5. *Examine communications systems very carefully, both outside systems and those in house.* Audit software may be needed to trace computer transactions. Call-back protection procedures may need to be installed: An effective call-back system will acknowledge a phone-in code, hang up, search its private directory, and then call the authorized number for that party.

6. *Do not use an outside electronic mail system unless it meets high standards of counterespionage control.* Many of these systems are not encrypted, and most have fairly weak controls. It may be wiser to use hand-delivered, authorized mail for highly sensitive information, such as product prototype proposals, demographic studies, and personnel reviews.

7. *Shield PC screens from unwanted eyes.* Because of its upright position, a computer screen is much easier to observe than paperwork lying flat on a desk or drawing table, especially at night and from a darkened area. A spy may be hundreds of feet away across the concrete canyons in any one of a dozen office buildings. Or the spy may be just outside the window on a wooded hillside or lurking behind a nearby file cabinet. If the eyes are windows to the human soul, then the computer screen is window to the soul of a company.

CHAPTER 9 ❓

Don't Bug Me:

Debugging and Electronic Countermeasures and Controls

> *"Even if you're on the right track, you'll get run over if you just sit there."*
> **Will Rogers**

Americans love technology. As one former Scotland Yard inspector put it: "The United States has technocrats instead of aristocrats. American technocracy takes the place of the English aristocracy."

Managers and executives have become more intimate with the world of electronics than the general population has because of the early and rapid growth of automation in the business environment. Understandably, they have used this knowledge in order to develop powerful tools and skills to help them in the war against corporate espionage. This chapter examines how managers deal with the threat of electronic bugs as well as how they protect themselves through on-site electronic surveillance and alarm systems.

DEBUGGING

Hand in hand with a love of technology comes a fear of technology. A nationwide survey that was first reported in 1981 (Craig Norback, *The Complete Book of American Surveys*, New York:

Signet Books, 1981) revealed that 85 percent of Americans seriously worry about illegal wiretaps and other forms of electronic spying. Here are some examples of how this love/fear relationship cuts across every aspect of the corporate culture.

■ The president of a service company decides to replace the cellular telephone in his company car. He buys the unit from Radio Shack and installs it himself. "It has twice the power of the one I had before," he explains, "and I can pull it out of the car and take it on the boat without waiting for a technician." The president hates to wait. He also hates to forget the details of an important meeting: He puts a fresh cassette in the recorder built into his briefcase.

The president is well aware that spies can also use these electronic gadgets to their benefit, so he's naturally concerned about his personal privacy and that of his top executives and managers. He should be! Security experts estimate that 100,000 small, wireless electronic bugs have been illegally planted in business offices within the last five years. The president himself is technically capable of planting and using a bug, which means he is also capable of performing basic debugging.

■ In the executive wing of a new office building the chief financial officer of another company sets up his own IBM desktop computer, linking it with the mainframe across town. Using a small, star-shaped screwdriver that looks like a piece of jewelry, he removes the cover of the PC so that he can get at the expansion slots. He then unpacks a plug-in communications board by slitting the carton with a high-tech, flat, black German pocketknife. Resembling an attractive key-ring ornament, it might be something an agent would carry when dropped behind enemy lines.

The CFO has the communications board plugged in, the software installed, and the system up and running within an hour. He is concerned about the possible presence of illegal wiretaps and other forms of electronic surveillance in his workplace. He is certainly capable of either basic bugging or basic debugging.

■ The resident expert on high-tech copy equipment in a government agency has taken several technical courses on her own. She now appears to understand the fundamentals of optical scanning as well as anyone. Aware of how easily technology can be employed to serve any end, she believes that electronic spying in the business world is far more prevalent than most surveys estimate. She admits that she has the know-how to plant and use a bug, and this means that she can also perform basic debugging.

The president who takes pride in maintaining his high-tech aids, the CFO who customizes his own PC, and the manager who keeps up with the latest developments in electronics all have a high degree of personal interest in what technology can do for and against them. They are especially sensitive to the threat of bugging. All businesspeople, however, need to become informed on this subject: Ignorance is the breeding ground for espionage.

Over the past twenty years, I have worked with a wide variety of people interested in electronic countermeasures, from West German engineers at Wurzburg Kaserne to East Coast executives and Silicon Valley engineers. They all ask the same questions. Here are the most frequent issues they raise.

Electronic Espionage Is Illegal: Do I Really Have to Worry About It?

Driving while intoxicated is also illegal, but people do it every day. There is less chance of being caught planting a bug! A few years ago, eavesdropping equipment was expensive and complicated. Only an expert with an important reason to do so was likely to bug an office, a residence, or a car. This is definitely not the case today. The equipment now available is cheap and easy to use, so office politics or just plain curiosity may be a strong enough motive for an employee to become an electronic spy. Statistics show that the rate of crimes featuring electronic espionage is skyrocketing. *Everyone* needs to be concerned.

Who Is Most Likely to Plant a Bug?

A spy can be anyone with a strong enough reason to spy. An office romance or business change that you consider minor may be a big deal to someone else. People who are interested in music systems, radio systems, or electronics in general have access to catalogs with lots of tempting do-it-yourself equipment. If they don't want to get personally involved in spying, they can always recruit another amateur or even a professional.

How Can I Determine My Level of Risk?

Even companies in the same field differ so much that risk levels are difficult to analyze. As a rule, however, it is the less tangible assets of a firm that are the most vulnerable to eavesdropping. The ideas expressed verbally during the course of forging a business plan or during a brainstorming session can be a company's most valuable assets and, of course, the ones most easily picked up by bugs.

Group meetings held in offices with outside walls accessible from a public area, or with windows facing office buildings across the street, run a strong risk of being bugged. So do casual chats with associates in the locker room of a local health club, where a bug and a voice-activated tape recorder can easily be stashed behind the vents of a locker!

What Circumstances Suggest That a Bug Might Be Present?

Aside from unusual electronic noises in a phone line or in a residence, office, or car, the most common early indicator of possible surveillance is a maddeningly subtle one: a queasy feeling, a dim intuition, a vague idea. It is worthwhile to remember that some of the shrewdest business decisions result from paying attention to those sixth-sense signals!

Usually the signal occurs when a manager is going through a major change at work (a new job, new research, new projects, new markets, new financial arrangements) or at home (a new residence, a divorce, a property settlement). Managers sometimes think only in terms of the company when considering business espionage controls and countermeasures. They fail to appreciate that it is often when their *personal* life is in turmoil that spies are most likely to target them for *business* espionage purposes. A divorce, for example, may change where a manager lives, whom the manager sees socially, and many other aspects of a daily routine.

All these changes give a spy a number of golden opportunities to infiltrate the manager's world and plant a bug in it.

The initial signal that something is amiss becomes clearer and more credible if co-workers, associates, or strangers seem to be behaving suspiciously. For example:

- A sales rep who also sells to a rival firm calls and wants to see your new office or factory or product line so she can "better serve your needs."
- Unidentified service people appear at your front door with tools and a story that does not quite ring true but is difficult to check.
- A rival co-worker goes in and out of your office after hours, for no apparent reason.

One of the manager-victim's first *tangible* clues of electronic surveillance is a small but inexplicable physical difference in the office or home environment. It could be that several objects are slightly out of place or rearranged. It could be that new items have been unobtrusively introduced—harmless-looking, even when inspected closely, but still unfamiliar and somehow unsettling.

What Is the Best Protection Against Electronic Espionage?

If you think you have been targeted for business espionage, take action immediately. If you don't have enough information to trigger a police investigation or a private security probe, you should definitely take the following steps:

1. *Assume your suspicions are true and begin treating the threat as you would any other threat to your business or personal privacy: Identify all risks, assess the potential damage, and develop appropriate countermeasures.* Your initial plan may be small and sketchy, but it will serve as a good basis for later additions and clarifications.

2. *Keep a log of unusual events in a small notebook or pocket calendar that you carry with you at all times.* Be specific in your notations: List names, times, dates, license numbers of suspected vehicles, and so on.

3. *Put "door checks," "drawer checks," and other simple checks in place as needed.* Slip a small piece of folded paper or cardboard in an office door where it will fall out if the door is opened during your absence. Private security guards often put a door check below the lock of every door they patrol during their first round of the evening. In this way, they won't walk in unprepared during the next round if a burglar or spy has entered with a stolen key.

These simple precautions can be surprisingly effective. In an interstate shipping case that focused on whether a warehouse door was being opened after hours, the telltale door check led to a three-state surveillance by FBI agents and private investigators, plus the recovery of truckloads of merchandise.

4. *Get professional help as soon as you have something to go on.* In a serious situation (one where life or limb may be in jeopardy), call the police *first.*

DO-IT-YOURSELF DEBUGGING

Unless you're a fairly competent electronic technician, it almost always makes more sense to rely on experts for debugging. Nevertheless, there are some simple debugging techniques you can apply on your own.

As noted in Chapter 4, the professional spy uses a wide range of electronic bugs. Much of this equipment is available to the general public, but some of the best is not: It is designed or redesigned by the spies themselves. Here are some of the most commonly used bugs and the debugging procedures for tracking them down.

Picking Up Transmitting Bugs

When most people think of bugs, they are specifically thinking of transmitting devices: miniature radio stations that broadcast live to a remote eavesdropper. Small bugs can be built into almost anything (such as an executive desk set) but they don't have much range. Larger bugs can transmit much farther and are also pretty easy to conceal. For example, a good-size bug can fit inside a desk clock. If the clock plugs into the wall, the bug has a permanent power supply. This is a bonus to the spy, since a dead battery is what puts most bugs out of action.

To locate a transmitting bug, you need a receiver. Most receiving devices designed for this purpose are rather expensive. They include:

- Surveillance receivers and spectrum analyzers for searching many frequencies to find the one the bug is transmitting on ($5,000 to $50,000).

- "Broom" and "dust mop" detectors (which look like mine detectors) for sending out signals to activate and energize the solid-state components in a wide variety of bugs, even when the bugs are turned off ($10,000 and up).

- Diode detectors, the most common and least effective bug-nabbers, which are not much more than an updated version of the old-fashioned crystal set ($100 and up).

There is a simple, far less expensive debugging mechanism that you can assemble yourself for locating audio transmitters. It won't catch the more sophisticated bugs, but it is operationally valid as far as it goes and is probably better than the diode detectors. The mechanism uses a portable TV set and a portable FM radio as electronic probes.

Your TV set and FM radio receive signals at different frequencies. Since every transmitting bug is a miniature broadcasting station, all you need to do is tune it in. Of course, you don't know at what frequency the bug is set, so you have to work the TV and radio dials between the normal stations and listen for the "feedback effect." Feedback occurs when the bug picks up the sound of your radio or TV and transmits it back again. The sound builds up again, is picked up again, and so on, until the noise gets so loud it howls or screeches from the speaker of your radio or TV.

Assume you want to test your office for bugs using this technique. First of all, remember not to talk about bugs or debugging in any area you think may be bugged! Then, turn off the TV set and everything else electrical in the room (except the lights) to cut down on distractions or background noise. Pull out the radio antenna full length, and turn on the radio to a comfortable listening level. Beginning at the low end of the dial, slowly move from station to station while you pass the telescoping antenna of the radio close to the walls, the floor, the ceiling, and the furniture. Ignore the stations themselves: It's the clandestine ministations between the regular ones that you're seeking. Run all the bands (frequency ranges) if your FM radio is multiband.

When you are finished with the radio, use a portable TV the same way. Pull the antenna out full length and set the VHF channel selector at the low end of the dial. Disconnect the cable TV connection if one is attached. Switch on the set and slowly revolve the fine-tuning knob as far as it goes in one direction and then the other while you run the antenna close to the walls, the floor, the ceiling, and the furniture. Repeat the process for each channel on VHF. Then do the same with the UHF channels.

When your radio or TV comes close to the frequency at which the bug is operating, you should start hearing the feedback effect. In the case of the TV, you may get "wiggle lines" across the screen instead of, or in addition to, the audio distortion. Be sure to turn the volume down when the noise level begins to rise so you won't alert the eavesdropper.

You may want to leave the bug in place for a while, if only to put the spy off guard. In the meantime, sharpen your own strategy and try to figure out a way to force the spy into the open. Be sure to consult an attorney if you have legal questions, but think twice about mentioning the bug to anyone else!

One more note: It's a good idea to have a cover story when you're performing a debugging procedure in case you are unexpectedly interrupted. I learned this the hard way during a debugging assignment for a corporate client in another city. When the airline misplaced my equipment en route, I was forced to rely on a portable TV and an FM radio to locate any audio transmitters. The client's facilities could not have been more poorly arranged, at least from the standpoint of security. The main building was entirely surrounded by parking lots and landscaped areas. Corporate offices were on the first floor, with the communications center in one corner and the boardroom in another. The conference table in the boardroom was within 10 feet of an outside wall with unrestricted parking only 20 feet beyond. I had visions of an under-the-table bug transmitting to a parked car outside even as the company executives were debating whether to use my services.

Checking out my vision, I was sprawled beneath the conference table with a TV and radio when the janitor walked in!

The janitor saw my feet sticking out underneath the table and bent down to see what I was doing. A bit miffed that the client had not mentioned it was clean-up night, I tried to maintain confidentiality by flipping the TV to a late-night talk show and grinning back at the janitor, as if I were an employee who always watched TV under a table. I eventually did find the bug where I suspected. I went back home, reported to the client, and moved on to other assignments. A few weeks later, the client called and reported that the janitor was taking his midnight lunch breaks with his own TV under the conference table. When questioned about it, the janitor swore that the reception there was better than anywhere else in the building!

Counteracting Nontransmitting Bugs

The nontransmitting bug listens or watches electronically but does not send what it hears or sees over the airwaves. It is often used in combination with a hidden recorder, or with a miniature television camera and a videotape machine. These devices can be devilishly small: A single unit consisting of a pinhole microphone and an audio recorder, for example, may be no bigger than a pack of cigarettes. An audio telescope (high-gain directional microphone), beloved by spies and bird-watchers alike, is another type of nontransmitting bug that can be used alone or with a recorder.

Many telephone taps are nontransmitting devices. Some attach to the wires along the line and record what is said. The most modern ones (such as the so-called proximity taps) pick up electrical impulses without even touching the wires themselves.

Nontransmitting devices are much more difficult to locate than transmitting devices, but there are simple measures to reduce their effectiveness. The best defense against nontransmitting audio devices is the age-old maneuver in spy thrillers: Turn on a radio for camouflage.

An audio tape recorder cannot distinguish between a live voice and a voice speaking on the radio at the same volume. There are sophisticated techniques for separating the two on tape. In most cases, though, if you leave the radio or TV running and speak near it you will make life wretched for buggers. In the Electronic Age, "Speak softly and carry a big stick" has become "Speak softly and carry a big radio to generate background noise."

Nontransmitting video bugs have to depend on available light, since video buggers usually cannot install studio lighting without alerting their victims (except, perhaps, in the fashion and entertainment industries). For this reason, spies frequently do what they can in the target locations to increase light levels subtly. They may put stronger bulbs in the lamps or add extra lamps to the room. Check out the lighting around you, and be suspicious of stronger-than-necessary lighting or lamps that suddenly appear in your normal working environment.

Making a Physical Search

A careful physical search may locate many types of bugs. Keep in mind that a bug may resemble something else, but a 9-volt battery looks like a battery. When you find one tucked away, just follow the wires.

Be methodical in your search for bugs and other listening devices. Obtain photocopies of floor plans so that you can make notes as you go along without writing on the originals. Use graph paper, personalized checklists, a portable computer, or anything else you are comfortable with to record your activities as accurately as possible. Maintain a written record of "who, what, when, where, how, and why."

During the search, don't throw objects around. Leave "tossing the room" to TV and movie dramatizations, where action is all-important. If you do toss the room, you will only have a mess on your hands and cover up more than you find. You will also tell whoever is watching and/or listening that you are suspicious.

You might disguise your search by pretending you are cleaning or redecorating your office or home. A vacuum cleaner sounds normal to an eavesdropper and gives you a good excuse for disturbing everything in the room one piece at a time. As you come to each object, move it, examine it carefully, and put it back exactly as you found it.

Don't overlook the obvious. Old-fashioned telephone taps at

the basement junction box and old-fashioned bugs that are nothing more than extension phones are still being used—mostly by old-fashioned spies!

If you proceed systematically, you should be able to find an object as small as a transistor battery, which is about as much as you can expect on your own. Professional controls and countermeasures experts rely on special training and experience to find the bugs you can't. Here are some of the questions that these professionals ask themselves when they begin any physical search for bugs:

■ *Where are people most likely to congregate?* By a particular desk or drafting table? By a telephone or office machine? By a coffee maker? The more "people factors" a specific setting has, the more likely a spy is to use it. In business espionage, a telephone in a lounge area is a natural for a bug, especially if it is a pay phone, which people feel is safer to use.

■ *Where is the best lighting in the room?* People have a natural tendency to move toward the light, and well-lit areas are the best places to read and discuss business papers.

■ *Do the suspected premises touch other premises?* It may be easier for a spy to poke a spike mike through from above, below, or next door than to enter the target office or residence. One area may have good alarms and security checks that the adjoining areas lack.

■ *Are the premises next to public areas?* A janitor's closet in the hallway just outside an office may be open twenty-four hours a day to anyone wearing overalls. Spies often pose as janitors, installers, and repairpeople. They may also pretend to take care of potted plants or wash windows or perform countless other special services. Spies even have printed "pretext manuals" describing service and repair schemes in detail.

■ *Does the potential victim do business in other environments besides the office?* In a car? On a boat? At poolside, over a cordless phone? (The cordless phone is a transmitter open to anyone listening on its frequency, unless the phone has its own code or other protection.) People tend to be more relaxed and to worry less about their privacy when they are away from the office. Spies know this and capitalize on it.

Nine Guidelines for Debugging

Any debugging program is a venture into the murky deep. Nine basic guidelines, culled from a long and successful career in electronic controls and countermeasures, can help uncloud the waters:

1. *Be positive in your approach to debugging.* Bugging is illegal under most circumstances. Debugging isn't. The spy is the one who should have a guilty conscience, not you. With this in mind, don't talk while the debugging process is under way: Let the spy sweat a little, wondering whether it is you, a janitor, the police, or the FBI making noises in the bugged area.

2. *Adopt a low-key strategy, at least at first.* If you suspect one particular person of bugging you, try to force that person out in the open. Do not mention your feelings to anyone, but observe the person closely until you are more confident of your suspicions. At this point, you might try a subtle squeeze.

For example, when the suspect enters the room where you think the bug is planted, position yourself so you can see his or her eyes. Then say casually, "I think my office may be bugged," as you move some papers to create a small distraction. If your suspicions are right, it will be almost impossible for the spy not to look at the spot where the bug is planted. Don't read too much into such a gesture right away, but by all means check out the spot when your suspect leaves.

3. *Look beyond the office.* The "look beyond" rule is so often forgotten, with such adverse consequences, that it bears repeating. If possible, always debug the closest telephone that might be perceived as safe. Businesspeople who duck out of the office to use the phone in the lobby for confidential discussions may well be using the phone most likely to be bugged! One "reformed" spy made this point rather colorfully:

> If some dude is going to call his bookie or his girlfriend, he goes to the closest outdoor phone. He passes on some insider information from there. He asks his buddy for hot tips from there. He lies through his teeth to his boss or his wife from there. You want to hear the human animal at its worst, just bug the nearest outside pay phone!

As for indoor phones, sharp guys pick the right phones, at least what appear to be the right phones—the ones in the quiet corners of the lobby or down the hall where they can see people coming and lower their voice. They gotta feel safe, even if they aren't really safe. I can tell the hot spots just by walking through a building, but every building is different. You can bet your assets that the public phones around any financial center are hot during breaks and right after work. Not only that, but they're the easiest to bug. If you're bugging an office, you gotta have a reason to be there. Who needs a cover to step up to a public phone?

4. *Don't get paranoid about bugging, but keep on the alert.* Be wary of "setups"—prearranged meetings, conferences, or conversations in which you are suddenly left alone. Statements like the following should make you cautious: "Stay put! I'll leave you people to talk it over." "Feel free to call your office! Use the phone in our conference room." Most people are honest and most business courtesies are genuine; but when important negotiations are under way, it is wise to be cautious.

5. *Take careful note of changes in your personal environment.* Spies are quite adept at using "masking techniques" to conceal espionage, so check out even the most apparently innocent changes in the objects, sounds, or lighting around you. A new window blind may contain a tiny listening device in one of the slats—an ideal position for transmitting what it hears through the window. Prerecorded construction noises may cover the sounds of forced entry or bug installation.

6. *Check out any stranger's cover story.* Spies use many legitimate-sounding explanations for why they are on the premises. For example, almost anyone can pose as a photographer and almost any bugging device can be hidden in camera gear. Graduate students, interns, and researchers are common interlopers in business environments, and spies can easily get printed credentials to pass themselves off in these roles. Don't hesitate to challenge strangers and to verify what they say with independent inquiries.

7. *Take a mental leap when you first think about possible bugging problems and solutions.* The beginning of any project is the time to generate as many creative ideas as you can—before you commit yourself to specific actions that confine your attention to closer limits. You can always resort to a more routine, grunt-

and-grind action plan if your initial brainstorming does not pay off.

Researchers in Britain have spent many years trying to locate ancient Roman forts by digging through historical documents. During a drought a few years ago, someone thought big and took to the air. The researcher figured out that buried ruins, even those plowed over in cultivated fields, would hold moisture better than the surrounding soil, so plants directly above them would stay greener longer. This phenomenon, the researcher gambled, would make the outlines of ruins visible from the air when all other vegetation had dried out. The researcher was right, and his mental leap saved future researchers many hours of trudging through musty archives and dusty fields.

The same leap of imagination can be of great benefit in finding much smaller buried caches, such as electronic bugs. Take a mental walk all around your environment. First, consider your business facility as a whole, perhaps with the aid of blueprints and architectural drawings or models. Look at it from above, from below, from the front, from the back, and from all sides. Then ask: "Where are the weak spots? If I were a spy, where might I want to plant audio bugs? Video bugs? What routes would allow me to penetrate the facility?" Follow the same 360-degree approach in your office, your home, or any other place you routinely conduct business.

Trace specific business systems or work flow patterns in the same manner. In reviewing telephone systems, for example, ask yourself: "Are the cables from the telephone company exchange strung from pole to pole as they come into the premises, or are they underground? Are they accessible at some point just off the premises and out of my control? Are telephone company service boxes accessible to outsiders either on the pole where the telephone lines are connected or at a terminal box in the building, or both?"

The point of this type of thinking is to raise your level of awareness so you can deal concretely with a normally invisible menace. One plant manager happened to notice a man open a telephone service box on a pole outside his office window. Because the manager had already visualized his facility with countermeasures and controls in mind, the sight stirred him to act. He called out to the man, who immediately climbed down and left the area.

Follow-up calls to the telephone company and to the local police failed to resolve the mystery, but the phone company's check on the service box did uncover a half-installed bug!

Chess and business (like chess and war) are often compared. As the business world becomes more complex, you must learn to play three-dimensional chess in analyzing your security risks. Simultaneously, there may be games going on above you, and all around you.

8. *Try not to jump to conclusions on the basis of incomplete information. One missing fact can change everything.* You have to be very careful about accusing someone of being a spy. One false move and you can easily fumble the ball. You may get the right person, but the wrong motive; and if you speak or act too soon, you may never uncover the real motive. The same can happen if you have the right motive but the wrong person. It's like the old Ike-and-Mike patter:

"Does your dog bite?"

"No."

(*Growl, growl, bite, bite.*)

"I thought you said your dog didn't bite!"

"That's not my dog."

Benny Hill, the English comedian, sums it up very well: "To ASSUME too much makes an ASS out of U and ME."

9. *Remember that a bug may be only one part of a much more extensive espionage campaign.* Electronic eavesdropping devices are not always used by themselves. The bug you find may be only the butterfly sipping the crocodile's tears. The real danger could lie much deeper in the mud.

It is important to keep this fact in mind *wherever* you conduct business. Even seminars and other study groups are becoming major arenas for complex business espionage operations. A typical scenario goes like this: A master spy contacts a mailing list broker to get a list of names in a particular target group—for example, "accountants in firms with government contracts," "award-winning research and development lab technicians," "middle managers belonging to X, Y, and Z professional societies."

Armed with this mailing list, organizer spies then plan a seminar. They arrange for speakers through a trade association (so the speakers will have no reason to question the legitimacy of the en-

terprise), rent space (or convince a company in their target industry to donate space), and send out invitations.

At the seminar itself, worker spies pose as attendees. The
speakers unwittingly direct interest to areas pinpointed by the
master spy, and the worker spies deliberately stimulate pertinent
conversation in the informal discussion groups and mixers that
follow—all held in bugged areas.

The bugged areas, then, represent the "front line" of the spy
operation—and a formidable line it is. Even if one bug is detected,
participants will probably think that the spy maneuver begins and
ends there—that the planted bug is a one-shot raid made by a
"legitimate" participant or a lone spy working for any one of innumerable companies with a special interest in the seminar or one
of its participants.

My advice to seminar attendees is to *gather* information at a
seminar rather than *give* it. Before I join any discussion group, I
make a point to research the areas I'm interested in so that I can
make a meaningful contribution. That's only fair. It isn't fair to be
asked to reveal specific details about my particular business.

SURVEILLANCE AND ALARM SYSTEMS

This chapter has been primarily devoted to finding (and outwit-
ting) electronic bugs, which pose a growing threat to unwitting
managers. But this is not the end of the manager's defense. Knowledgeable managers can also thwart spies *before* they get a chance
to plant their bugs by installing electronic surveillance and alarm
systems in the office, factory, or home. Prevention, after all, is the
better part of debugging!

ELECTRONIC SURVEILLANCE: THE BIG BROTHER DILEMMA

Closed-circuit TV systems that observe customers in stores and
trespassers in warehouses rely on the same miniature cameras that
spies use. The cameras can be out in the open or concealed in any

of the ways that spies conceal them. The same goes for audio transmitters, many of which can double as intercoms.

Every manager has free rein to turn these weapons against *outside* spies at critical entrances and exits to an office, factory, or residence. But what about internal surveillance? Serious ethical problems can arise when electronic surveillance is used to monitor employee activities.

At United Technologies Corporation (UTech), 1984 was a truly Orwellian year. UTech's board of directors was forced to begin investigating charges that its chairman, Harry Gray, had bugged two former executives. In the course of its investigation, the board assembled evidence of numerous other management-directed bugging campaigns in the recent past.

That same ominous year, a group of sixteen UTech employees filed suit, claiming that company management had engaged in widespread bugging to gather inside information about employee plans to form a union. "Corporate espionage is par for the course over there," complained James Kestrell, a lawyer for the group. Charles Tracy, a UTech machinist, commented, "You have to believe we've either been bugged or tapped because they have such an up-to-date and accurate account of what takes place in the union hall."

Nothing has been proved yet against UTech. Thomas Bouchard, UTech's vice-president of industrial relations, says that the company management usually does know what's going on among its employees, but adds, "That's because we keep in touch with our people and try to understand what's in their hearts and minds." Nevertheless, the mere suggestion of clandestine electronic surveillance has damaged morale among UTech employees, turned employees against UTech leadership, and tarnished UTech's public image.

The allegations against UTech are serious because they involve clear violations of an employee's right to privacy. Much less clear-cut in implication are the increasingly popular monitoring devices for measuring employee productivity. By installing computer software in a central computer, employers can monitor everything from how well clerical personnel accomplish quantifiable tasks on their PCs to what specific transactions management personnel are performing on their PCs.

Experts estimate that more than a third of the 13 million

Americans who work on office PCs are monitored. According to Michael Smith, professor of industrial engineering at the University of Wisconsin, "By the year 2000, there will be 30 to 40 million [PC] users and as many as 50 to 75 percent of them will be monitored."

Another common form of management-initiated electronic eavesdropping involves bugging telephone lines to check the quality of customer service. At present, this technique is directed primarily at lower-level jobs. But as the software technology becomes more sophisticated, almost any in-house phone conversation can become an open conduit to management.

Employees are usually told in advance that they are being monitored. When they aren't told, they usually find out eventually. If nothing else, awareness that this type of relentless scrutiny is going on can sap a worker's spirit and creativity. Harley Shaken, professor of labor and technology at the University of California (San Diego), remarks, "Monitoring combines nineteenth-century forms of labor relations with twentieth-century technology, creating the discipline of an electronic assembly line."

What worries many people, of course, is that overeager employers will extend the possibilities of electronic eavesdropping far beyond the boundary separating performance evaluation from invasion of privacy. Edwin Sherin, senior vice-president of operations for American Express, offers this advice to managers who entertain the idea of electronic surveillance of their employees: "Don't surprise people or use monitoring as a club to catch them. Let them know what's going on and why. Giving employees access to the data you gather and the procedures for challenging erroneous records can also break down suspicions."

ALARM SYSTEMS: ELECTRONIC ALLIGATORS FOR CASTLE AND MOAT

A good electronic alarm system is vital to the security of any office, factory, or home. Best of all, the person responsible for installing the system doesn't have to worry about stirring up any ethical controversies! There are two basic types of alarm systems: perimeter alarms (often referred to as point-of-entry alarms), which *sur-*

round the area to be protected, and space alarms, which are set up *inside* the area.

It is obviously better to have an alarm that goes off while an intruder is trying to get in than an alarm that triggers only after the intruder is inside. The two types of alarm systems overlap to a degree, however, and may be used together or separately. Some single units serve as both perimeter and space alarms. As with most one-size-fits-all products, it is wise to check carefully on how well they can adapt to particular needs.

Both types of alarms send signals to either "local" or "central station" systems when the alarm is tripped. In local alarm systems, bells, horns, flashing lights, or other warning devices are placed on the protected premises. In central station systems, the signal travels over the telephone line to a private security organization that either sends its own agent immediately to the premises (ideally!) or notifies the police. In the latter case, a police officer may phone the premises instead of responding in person: False alarms are common, and often police departments do not have enough time and personnel to respond to each call, except perhaps in very small or very affluent communities.

Central station alarm systems are generally more expensive than local alarm systems, and they still need to be supplemented by a local alarm. It is all very well to send for outside help, but the person prying open your patio door with a tire iron needs to know that the disturbance has been discovered before any damage is done!

Perimeter Alarms

Perimeter alarms are a first line of defense. In its simplest (and most common) form, a perimeter alarm is a wired system consisting of a bell, a battery or some other power source, and switches attached to doors and windows in such a way that the bell rings when any one door or window is opened.

A complete system includes a backup power supply, a control panel, and a way of testing circuits without sounding the alarm. There may also be a time-delay switch that allows for exit or entry within a preset time limit without triggering the alarm.

Variations on this basic system include such streamlined

mechanisms as narrow strips of electrified metallic foil that are glued to windows as part of the alarm circuit. There are also wireless alarm systems, which are rapidly gaining popularity over wired alarm systems. A wireless system uses one or more small radio transmitters to trigger the alarm. The alarm can be set off by pressing a button on a portable transmitter—a distinct advantage to someone who walks in on an emergency situation.

There are three basic types of perimeter alarms: photoelectric, laser, and vibration. Photoelectric alarms use infrared beams to form an alarm network: Any break in the light beam sets off the alarm. Laser perimeter systems use laser beams in place of infrared beams to extend the range of the alarm. In vibration alarm systems, sensors attached to the inside of windows and doors are activated by vibration. A major problem with vibration systems is that passing trucks and planes or flying debris can easily trigger a false alarm. At home, where bump-and-tussle accidents can happen frequently, such systems may prove self-defeating. It may be wiser to attach a short black wire to a suction cup, stick the cup to the inside of a window for its deterrent effect, and buy some other alarm system!

Space Alarms

Space alarms are most often used indoors, although they too have broad applications both indoors and out. Space alarms work best when the premises are vacant, since they don't permit occupants to retire behind a "moat" as perimeter alarms do. There are three major varieties of space alarms: ultrasonic, microwave, and capacitance.

Ultrasonic space alarms are set to detect an intruder's movements in a vacant room or office. They are often disguised as stereo speakers, books, or other low-profile items. An ultrasonic space alarm's high sensitivity to any disturbance in the cubic area of its range makes it an excellent protective mechanism, but it also can cause problems. Even an air conditioner can set it off if it's not adjusted properly. One executive who installed an ultrasonic space alarm at home had numerous false alarms when his dog went in and out through a pet door that he kept forgetting to lock. These alarms can be set so that they won't go off unless an intruder the size of a human being enters the scene.

Microwave alarms detect motion by generating a force field. They are more expensive than ultrasonic systems and just as vulnerable to false alarms. Their advantage is that they can be even more finely tuned to discriminate among intruding agents.

Capacitance alarms are used on safes, file cabinets, storage boxes, and other ungrounded metallic objects. A change in the electrical field when someone approaches sets off the alarm. This "closeness" factor accounts for the other, less common name for these devices: proximity alarms. The advantage of the capacitance alarm is that its range can be confined to a very precise location, so that nonintruders can more easily move around adjacent areas when it is operating.

Any alarm system will need service from time to time, so it is only as good as the company that backs it. The less you know about burglar alarms, the more you need expert advice from a reliable supplier. The time to check on an alarm supplier is before you buy!

Most burglar alarm companies provide good support for their products, but the field is growing so fast that there are some exceptions. One firm in my neighborhood seems to be little more than a sales organization with a telephone answering service. It offers a good contract on its equipment but can never be reached "in person." I left a three-page list of questions concerning one product on the company's answering machine tape, but have yet to receive a reply. I'm not holding my breath, and neither would a burglar!

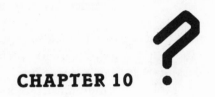

CHAPTER 10

Who *Will* Be Stealing
Your Business?

The Espionage Boom Ahead
and How to Halt It

> *"In the first half of this century,
> Mr. Justice Brandeis called privacy
> the right most valued by civilized
> men. In the last half of this
> century, we must make it the right
> that is most protected."*
> **Richard M. Nixon**

Business venturers have always made complicated efforts to see into the future, from Stone Age pelt peddlers who foretold market success by reading entrails to Computer Age electronic wizards who program demographic fractal projections on their laptop PCs. Unfortunately, no crystal ball, electronic or otherwise, is needed to predict the future of corporate spying: In the coming years, it is certain to undergo explosive growth.

What is the reason for this gloomy state of affairs? Why is espionage booming? How can American business survive in such a dangerous new world? The answers to these questions are the focus of this chapter.

THE ESPIONAGE BOOM

Spy technology has become a major industry, leading to increasingly sophisticated products and an ever expanding public interest. Not long ago, advertisements for surveillance equipment could be found only in trade periodicals, gun-and-adventure rags, and a miscellaneous (not to mention motley) assortment of underground publications. Today, ads for such equipment appear regularly in mass-market magazines, promoting surveillance gear as "executive tools," "communications aids," "protection insurance," or simply "high-tech toys."

One such ad offers plans for building a listening device with parts available at neighborhood electronics stores. Radio Shack parts numbers are correlated with the resistors, capacitors, diodes, and transmitters needed to assemble the bug. Exact specifications and suppliers are listed for the perfboard mounting, the type and gauge of wire, and the best kind of soldering iron. There are even multiview photos to accompany the schematic how-to drawings! The finished device—smaller than the 9-volt battery that powers it—has a range of over 700 feet. And it's easy enough for the proverbial child to assemble. As one teenager commented: "Sure, I can make that! All you have to do is take the shopping list to the mall and then follow the instructions!"

In one issue of *Popular Science* alone, ads appeared for (1) a bug catalog, (2) a new cubic-inch, line-attachable gadget that records telephone conversations, and (3) a miniature four-stage FM transmitter not much bigger than a 9-volt battery that can pick up whispers 50 feet away and broadcast up to 1 mile. Several other fast-selling items on the cutting edge of spy technology are promoted from time to time in a variety of magazines: tiny solid-state "chip" cameras, fiber-optic lenses, and "repeater stations" that can pick up the signal of a small transmitter, intensify it, and pass it on to a much greater range.

In the future, technological developments are destined to increase both the spread of corporate espionage and the capabilities of individual spies.

The Thoughtful Computer

Computers will be refined to perform more and more complex intelligence-gathering tasks—to the benefit of both legitimate and illegitimate users. The National Security Agency reportedly has computers that key on specific words or phrases in a telephone conversation and automatically record the call. Similar computers that can respond to human voice commands will soon be available to everyone—including the corporate spy!

Software, too, poses new risks. Independent computer whizzes of dubious ethics will be able to use advanced software programs to track and manipulate data banks in more and more subtle ways. Setting themselves up as "information brokers," they can offer services to their clients that range all the way from basic market research to detailed blueprints for crime.

Finally, there are the staggering implications of artificial-intelligence (AI) interfacing. In simple terms, AI software can enable a computer to distill *meaning* from data, so that the computer itself can "think" and make relevant cross-references in its data base. What now would take a spy (or a legitimate operator) weeks of both mental and computer work to achieve might soon take an AI-driven computer a few hours. Indeed, the AI-driven computer may be able to point out significant patterns, culled from thousands of pieces of data, that would be impossible for one human mind to discover in a lifetime.

"Remote" Possibilities

Talking advertising signs, first introduced on California highways in the early 1980s, are now popping up across the nation. These signs bid passing motorists to tune their radios to a particular frequency so that they can hear a recorded sales pitch, broadcast from a transmitter built into the sign itself. These signs and similar marketing devices now making their appearance will quickly familiarize a vast number of businesspeople with the wonders of electronic transmission, for both legal and illegal uses.

Night-vision infrared imaging systems are capable of sensing the difference in temperature between an object and its background and then projecting the image of the object on a remote monitor. This is only one approach to the problem of seeing in the dark, but one that General Motors is aggressively investigating for commercial applications: A night-vision monitor may soon be mounted on the dashboard of every car!

Spies already see in the dark with the help of light enhancers. It's a good bet that they will be using "legal" infrared imaging systems to avoid company guards on night patrol long before these systems become standard automobile equipment.

Before the end of the century, remote-control aircraft—from small model planes to full-size "drones"—will more effectively employ a wider range of cameras and bugs to spy on corporate targets. The military has already pioneered the use of RPVs (remotely powered vehicles) to conduct foreign espionage, and the private sector will now start to catch up with it.

The technology is definitely in place and available. Much of it is well within the budget and know-how of even the poorest and most mechanically inept would-be spy. One photographer bought a toy remote-control tank, attached a miniature camera and tape recorder to it, and used it to take dramatic close-ups of birds moving across the desert floor—pictures so good that they appeared in *National Geographic*. The very same toy tank with its store-bought miniature camera and tape recorder could just as easily go under the back fence of a business enterprise and be "the bug that plants itself."

Robotics

Robotic devices will soon play a major part in business espionage. The British army used a rather crude little security robot in Northern Ireland as early as 1973. It was built like a miniature truck, could climb stairs, and carried a television camera and a remote-control, five-round shotgun. It disarmed bombs, opened car trunks, towed vehicles, and performed other hazardous duties without once malfunctioning.

Descendants of this guerrilla robot are now being used for security purposes in airports, harbors, oil refineries, chemicals plants, and other high-risk areas around the world. One robot at Boston's Bayside Exposition Center uses mobile microwave sensors to detect intruders during the graveyard shift.

Little tin people as talented and personable as R2D2 may still be a futurist's dream, but robots are far enough advanced to do most basic spy work. With closed-circuit TV eyes, minimicrophone ears, and computer brains, they can move their mechanical arms to perform a multitude of complex tasks. TV viewers who watched a robot explore the sunken *Titanic* can attest to a sophisticated robot's eerily human ability to maneuver in and out of tight places and find "the good stuff."

It is only a matter of time before robots become more prevalent demicitizens of the business world and (like their flesh-and-blood counterparts) potential corporate spies. Most robots are custom-made units with specialized electronic circuitry. Few people, even technicians, would be able to spot a well-placed bug in such a system. Moreover, many robots have backup power supplies that can be used to operate small, illegally embedded listening devices and cameras efficiently and invisibly.

There is an insidious sidelight to the use of robotics in espionage: People are far more likely to ignore nearby machines than they are nearby people. An electronic mail cart in an office complex could eavesdrop on the conversations of key management personnel much more effectively than a human being and without arousing suspicion. A robotic arm in a factory could unobtrusively photograph and record an entire production line each time it moved to recycle itself for the next part of its regular job, and none of its human "co-workers" would be any the wiser.

Fantasy has foreshadowed reality throughout history. The sci-fi movies and comics of today could prove correct: In the twenty-first century, the robot may indeed emerge as the ultimate secret agent!

MORALITY, ETHICS, AND EXAMPLE

How can businesspeople survive in a climate where espionage poses such a pervasive threat? The individual manager or business can reduce the odds of becoming victimized by staying informed of the ways and means of business espionage and maintaining appropriate controls and countermeasures. The only way for the business world in general to make headway in the war against business espionage, however, is *to promote and enforce moral and ethical restraints on spying.*

Morality and ethics must become stronger, more operative elements in business conduct, if only to keep pace with the rapid strides that "impersonal" technology is taking. Otherwise, the state of the electronic art will soon remove spies so far from the actual point of intrusion that they will lose sight of the gravity of what they are doing. Only history can provide an appreciation of how treacherous this situation is.

Evolution of a Spy

Before the Civil War, spying was basically a one-on-one activity, in which "right" and "wrong" could easily be given human faces. Things began to change quickly as the war fueled the growth of technology. The post–Civil War era presented Allen Pinkerton, founder of the country's first major "domestic secret service agency," with several brave new challenges.

In 1867, in one of his trickiest investigations, Pinkerton was hired to catch "invisible" spies who were tapping the telegraph lines of Western Union in an effort to manipulate the stock market. In a letter to his client, Pinkerton pointed out that the telegraph line would be an important part of business in the future and would require new security measures. "The lines must be protected by Congress," he wrote, "so that a man who stole communications from the wires was equally guilty as the man who stole letters out of the mail and opened them. . . ." (James D. Horan, *The Pinkertons—The Detective Dynasty That Made History,* New York: Bonanza Books, 1967, p. 153.)

Business spies and others willing to go outside the law would soon have enormously broader opportunities for wiretapping and eavesdropping. Pinkerton's statements were made less than ten years before Alexander Graham Bell's invention of the telephone. It is ironic that the first official telephone conversation in 1876 had eavesdroppers on the line as part of the public demonstration—a prophecy of things to come!

The twentieth century ushered in the Age of Radio. Marconi had worked with radio signals since 1895. Radio receivers were available in 1913, and radio telephones in 1915. By 1929, FM radio had become a reality. The world Pinkerton's followers were exploring was a radically more worrisome one. Public morality had *not* evolved in lockstep with technology, as most turn-of-the-century philosophers had hoped. Instead, technical advances were making it *easier* to sidestep moral issues!

Before radio, the spy had to take a personal risk to listen in on a conversation, a risk that acted as a built-in restraint to indiscriminate spying. After radio, the spy could eavesdrop from afar. Before radio, the spy had to zero in on one person, or one small group, to have any chance of success. The spy therefore needed irresistible evidence up front—a strong "cause" for spying—to justify the great expenditure of time and effort. After radio, the spy could easily take a scattershot approach to spying by switching from listening device to listening device, wavelength to wavelength, and band to band.

The addition of television and computer technology to the spy's repertoire has extended the scope of espionage operations and stretched the spy's conscience even further. As one modern-day business spy points out: "If you do enough listening, viewing, and random searching, sooner or later you will get *something* on *someone.*" The problem in this situation is that moral and ethical judgments are no longer put to the test of overt action. The spies of the past were forced to lay themselves on the line. Caught on their hands and knees with an ear to the keyhole, they found it difficult to convince themselves or anyone else that they were actually praying. Electronic technology enables modern spies to fool themselves and others—to say one thing and do another—because they are one step removed from the act.

The Amoral Amateur

Modern spies may not even possess a clear-cut intention to spy, one that would make them feel responsible for their acts. They may just be "fishing around" because it's convenient to do so. As the examples throughout this book have demonstrated, a very fine line separates legitimate from illegitimate information-gathering methods. In the future, this line could get even fainter, as people become more and more "techno-literate." In the future, too, as fishing around becomes even more convenient, the typical spy will most likely be an amateur rather than a professional.

Professional investigators often cite the absence of moral or ethical restraints among amateurs: "Amateur spies, amateur morals," they say. It is doubtful that amateurs have less active consciences than professionals; but amateur spies can more easily be seduced into committing individual acts of espionage. Their rationale may well be that since bugging equipment is available to everyone, it must be okay to use, and since spying is so easy that anyone can do it, they may as well try it themselves.

One data manager summed up the dilemma: "It's brutal! We're going through a reorganization and everyone is out for blood. My boss is acting so weird that I record everything she says to me on a pocket tape recorder, just in case I'm on her hit list and need to fight back."

Is the data manager going too far? Are his actions unethical? Perhaps paranoid?

It's getting more and more difficult to judge these situations, especially for people who have had no formal discussion with their peers, mentors, trainers, or employers about moral and ethical business conduct. Commenting about a similar incident in a recent issue of *Business Week,* Allen J. Frances, associate professor of psychiatry at Manhattan's Payne Whitney Clinic, notes that defensive spying "might be a perfectly normal thing to do. Some environments reward the meticulous person." Dr. Robert London of the New York University Medical Center remarks, "Unfortunately, we live in a world where people frequently try to manipulate one another, and there often is a real need to cover yourself."

The data manager would do well to consult with an attorney on the matter of taping his boss. The legal restrictions and penalties vary so much from place to place and incident to incident that even experts in law are frequently confused. Whatever the situation, however, the data manager is likely to gamble that he won't be prosecuted for using a pocket recorder. "Intent" under such circumstances is hard to prove; and these cases have low priority in most jurisdictions.

Another morally and ethically ambiguous situation involved a service manager who was convinced that his employees were being spied on by a competitor. "I know the bastard is following my sales reps around," he complained. "I see no reason why I shouldn't fight fire with fire and have him and his people followed. We spend big bucks developing leads, which he gets for free. I'm going to get some of his!"

Is the service manager going too far? Is what he is planning unethical?

I believe it is. The clue lies in his "fight fire with fire" analogy. He is thinking like an arsonist when he should be thinking like a fire fighter. If he took the time to brief his sales staff on business espionage controls and countermeasures, he could put out the fire, rather than add to it. When his staff started taking precautions, the problem would most likely diminish. He could also put his own people (not his rival's people) under protective surveillance by professional investigators for a few days. Professionals are better equipped to identify spies-in-action and they have no self-serving motive for checking out how a client's competitor operates.

Case History 8: The No Name Bar

Independent, cold-blooded, and committed amateurs may be relatively exceptional creatures today, but they are destined to be fairly common in the future. Their tools may be no bigger than a pack of cigarettes and their hideaway no more secret than the corner bar. A manufacturer facing problems with inventory control hired an experienced undercover agent to investigate. As is so often the case, the agent discovered a whole nest of problems centering around the local watering spa: the No Name Bar.

The No Name is a sanctuary for salespeople during the day— a hideaway just beyond the business district with several isolated telephones in back for making appointments and a row of sheltered booths along a side wall for catching up on paperwork. In short, it is an ideal office-away-from-the-office for the sales rep who is supposed to be out in the field, especially on Friday afternoons when most executives like to leave their companies early and seldom schedule high-level sales meetings.

One such afternoon, the undercover agent went to the No Name with two of his client's salesmen. Here is his account of what happened:

> *One of the men was sitting where he could see the door. It was obvious, at least to me, that he was looking for someone. Three men I didn't recognize arrived about that time and went to a booth in the back. The man who had been watching the door took what looked like an empty cigarette pack out of his*

pocket and said, "I'm going for smokes." When he passed the booth in the back, I saw him drop the cigarette pack into the fake foliage plants in the divider between the booths.

When the man returned to our table, he took an ordinary pocket radio from his briefcase, turned it on, and put the earphone speaker to his ear. I knew that the empty cigarette package that he had discarded near the booth in the back must have contained an FM bug, and that he was now listening in. The other salesman at the table asked, "What's the score?" The man with the radio said, "Nothing to nothing at the moment. If anything juicy happens, I'll let you know." I was really surprised—I've been an investigator for seven years and had never seen anyone plant a bug in public! I thought I must be on to something big.

The salesman with the radio eavesdropped until the three men in the back booth walked out, and then he retrieved the bug on his way to the toilet. I hung around with him during the next few days while another investigator who was not working undercover did background checks on the three men my man had bugged. We were very thorough, but came up empty. There was nothing unusual about my man, nothing at all. He wasn't spying for someone else. He wasn't in financial trouble, didn't use drugs, and wasn't under any special pressure at work. He just wanted to know what the competition was doing!

My man had been a salesman in the city since college and had seen the competition come and go. He would take a few customers away from them, and they in turn would steal a few from him. The score was about even until recently. He had lost more than his share of clients since the first of the year and had wondered why. He had also noticed that sales reps from the rival firm dropped into the No Name on Friday. It wasn't long until he decided to start spying on the competition. As we became better acquainted, he talked about it openly. He did not know, of course, that I was an investigator!

He thought, among other things, that the sales reps from the other company dressed better than he did and drove better cars—at his expense. He was sure they were stealing his accounts and saw nothing wrong with checking it out. Perhaps it was one part self-preservation, one part envy, and two parts curiosity that got him going. I don't know. I am sure he was not a professional. He wasn't spying for anyone but himself. If he does get caught bugging the competition, no doubt his *employer will suffer, but there isn't much chance he'll be caught. Even if they catch him, it would still be difficult for the other company to make a case. As far as I know, he's still operating at the No Name!*

In the end, the best *defense* against amoral business spies is what the Apache call "the way of watchfulness." The essence of business espionage controls and countermeasures, after all, is more a mind-set than a methodology. The best *offense* against corporate espionage, however, requires a more active role in defining, following, and disseminating moral and ethical codes for conducting business.

It's obvious that during the last two decades of unprecedented expansion in the corporate world, the tangible triumphs of business success have begun to outweigh the intangible values of a fair and honest business environment. This is an age when the name of a convicted felon in the Watergate scandal is used to promote a nationwide chain of private detective agencies; when an officer of the U.S. Information Agency can rationalize that highly classified government documents are only "low-level State Department chit-chat" and therefore can be passed on to known foreign agents; when business practices that an earlier generation would have condemned are publicly praised and admired on Wall Street, in *Fortune* magazine, and at Harvard Business School.

There are no hard-and-fast guidelines for establishing ethical business codes—much less for popularizing and enforcing them. If there were, spies could not flourish. What managers and executives need to do is begin with their own conduct and rigorously supervise it. They have to make individual commitments to respect the privacy of others and avoid fooling themselves into thinking that honorable ends justify dishonorable means, or that they have a right to do to other people what others do (or might do) to them. Only when managers are sure that they can distinguish between right and wrong conduct in their own sphere of operations can they be effective in communicating a similarly strong sense of ethics and morality to employees and business contacts.

Spies are parasites. They cannot thrive in a culture that doesn't feed them. It is up to every responsible manager and executive to put his or her house in order first and then take steps to protect that house, so that it can prosper and be a shining model for others in the community. Only through morality, ethics, *and* example can tomorrow's world become one in which espionage is not only much less popular but also much less profitable.

Index

scramblers, electronic, 135
second business, 44
secret operator, *see* undercover investigators
secretaries, executive, 42
security
  after-hours tour for, 79–86
  goals of, 78
  objectives of, 118, 119
security checklists, 118
  for factory, 97–105
security consultants, 31, 114–130
  and company security people, 116–117
security
  interviewing, 117–119
  locating, 128–129
  management knowledge of, 129
  role of, 119
  training of, 116
security guards, 78, 81
  armed, 102
  contract, 102
  in factory security checklist, 101–102
  rounds for, 82
  schedules of, 34
security industry, specialization in, 129–130
security information, theft of, 34–35
Security magazine, 4
security risks, 31
security surveys, 74
  do-it-yourself, 87–112
  planning, with consultants, 118–119
security systems, breaching, 68
security-walk-through model, 78
seminars, 13, 164–165
service companies, espionage risk in, 27–29

Service Corporation, 19, 20, 21
service technicians, 13
Shaken, Harley, 167
Sherin, Edwin, 167
Shevardnadze, Eduard, 57
shipping, 25
shipping area, in after-hours security tour, 84–85
shredders, 41–42
shrubbery, in security checklist, 88, 92
Sloane, Burt, 135
Smith, Michael, 167
social conversations, confidential information revealed in, 38
software, 81
  customized, and staff spying, 38
  for monitoring employee productivity, 166
  trends in, 173
Soldier of Fortune, 84
space alarms, 168, 169–170
specialists, and espionage risk, 21
specifications, as spy target, 18
spectrum analyzers, 156
spies
  business vs. government, 4–7
  characteristics of, 3–4
  confronting, 111–112
  covers for, 46
  environment for, 181–182
  ethics and, 15
  evolution of, 176
  insiders as, 36–56
  operating methods of, 7–10
  trash search by, 51–53
  undercover, 39–46
  use of electronic bugs by, 152–153
  vs. undercover investigators, 122
sports, 61